PEEK-A-BOO, I SEE YOU!

Parenting From Your Child's Point of View

By
SANDRA GUNN

InnerImages Books
Maryland

InnerImages Books
IIB
Since 1983

PEEK-A-BOO, I SEE YOU!
Parenting From Your Child's Point of View

For information address:
InnerImages Books
PO Box 5856
Annapolis, MD 21403

Editorial supervision by Dmitri Gunn
Illustrations by Pam Winterbottom
pdwinterbottom@yahoo.com

ISBN–13: 978-0-615-30051-1
ISBN–10: 0-615-30051-0

First Edition: December 2009
Printed in the United States of America

10 9 8 7 6 5 4 3 2 1

This book is dedicated to:

My Mother
She passed away on January 23, 2000
She lived with commitment.

My Father
He passed away on March 29, 1973
He lived with patience.

My Sons, Dmitri and Dakus
"There are no shortcuts to anyplace worth going."

Stephen
"No revenge is more honorable than the one not taken."

CONTENTS

INTRODUCTION

This book is about unexpected parenting. It is about the wondrous nature of childhood innocence and what they come here to teach us. It is about creating learning opportunities, which stimulate and expand curious minds. It is about home schooling in the formative years and the sacrifice and joy of family commitment. It is about lessons, about living, about loving, about faith, and about being human. It is mostly a book about being human and about learning from those we teach.

Children arrive with wide-eyed innocence, pure and dependent. They come to us with no expectations and no experience. We are their caretakers and their teachers. We are their examples, and they mimic us throughout their lives. We are their first chance and their last word. Children are for as long as we live.

Life's unexpected journeys with our children create an abundance of opportunities for growth. This book is about that growth – its joys and pain, its rewards and sacrifices. We begin child rearing by thinking we are in charge. We come to understand that it is a symbiotic relationship, parents and children teaching and learning from each other. There are no masters when we are all learning for the first time. We are all students.

This is a book about spiritual growth, whose recipe includes emotional pain and joy. Spiritual growth takes our lives from the mundane to the extraordinary. Without spiritual growth, there is no life; there is only existence. Without emotional pain, there is no joy; there is only stillness. It is the stillness that drives us mad.

Change is essential for growth. Every challenge and every risk is, at the end of the day, a test of each human's faith and what he or she is willing to sacrifice to stay true to that faith. Life is a test of faith. That is really all it is.

It is our curiosity and our thirst for answers that propels us into ourselves. All knowledge lives within us. I am fortunate to have lived in a place of serenity where I was able to hear myself. I went to bed with the crickets, woke up with the birds, and listened to my inner voices.

My test of faith wove a tapestry of joy with sorrow, love with sacrifice, and pain with healing; all of which sculpted me into the being that I am today. As I grew with my children, my world expanded and the dimmest lights in the smallest corners of my life began to illuminate a path to celebration. The light of this quiet faith freed me from the clamor and distractions of the manufactured world. It is comforting to know that this journey has only just begun. The road is long. There is no end, only the constant assurances of beginnings.

All journeys begin in the noise and end in the quiet. Solitude is a within thing. It may be felt in the middle of a crowded subway or on a noisy street. Inner solitude is worth the journey. Whatever it takes; it is worth the journey.

Life should be lived in Paradise. Paradise is here. I have often wondered why we thought it was somewhere else.

Sandra Gunn
November 11, 2008

PREFACE

Family requires two parents, a father and a mother. That is the definition of family – two parents and children. Although this book comes from my perspective, that of a mother, I could not have achieved the educational goals and our combined vision for our family without the dedication, support, and encouragement of the Father and his profound belief.

Not only was Stephen a loving, compassionate, and generous Father, he was always there to lift his sons when they fell and hold them close when they cried. He sacrificed his good so they could achieve theirs. His dedication to his family was extraordinary. He seemed to have an innate understanding of the bonds that held us all together, and this was of great comfort as we all sailed our little boats through the storms and calm of life. He was our glue, and he created our glow when things looked grey. His sense of humor filled our rooms with laughter, and his ability to stoop down low and look into their small, wide-open eyes made a lasting impression on their self esteem, as they sensed their equality by looking into his eyes and not up at them.

The Father was a very busy man and could not always participate physically in my stories. He was there with his support, and I was there doing the things I knew best to do. He gave his consent, approval, and financial backing to our adventures. He went along on our journeys and heartily participated in the educational experiences I conjured up, so our sons would have the greatest exposure to life that we were able to offer. He never discouraged but always encouraged our educational schemes: honey bees, grouse hunts, dinosaurs, guns, gardening, art, music, space camp, sailing, horseback riding, chickens, cats, dogs, Alger the black snake, Blue the crippled groundhog, little funerals, and even flying lessons! Yes, one day I came home and thought they should learn how to fly.

Stephen flew planes and understood the exhilaration of the sky, thunder storms, lighting, clouds, and freedom. I thought our sons should have this, too. While we could provide flying lessons, I did not want them to miss the experience. So we drove to the local airport twice a week and I sat on the ground as they took off with their flight instructors into the blue sky. Stephen would review their flight books each week to their great pride. He was always there and always open to their enthusiasm.

This book is a tribute to his endurance, love, and support. His sons are a tribute to his patient nurturing. They have his strength of conviction, dedication to justice, and love of family. He was central to the development of their defining themselves. We were a rowdy bunch, and he survived this amazing journey. For his perseverance, I respect, admire, and thank him.

There is no family without a Father and Mother.

DREAMCICLE CHILDREN

"As far as the education of children is concerned
I think that they should be taught not the little virtues
but the great ones.
Not thrift but generosity and an indifference to money;
not caution but courage and contempt for danger;
not shrewdness but frankness and a love of truth;
not tact but love for one's neighbor and self-denial;
not a desire for success but a desire to be and to know."

"The Little Virtues"
Natalia Ginzburg

THE BEGINNING

1. THE BEGINNING

I really did not want children. My own childhood was so confining and filled with responsibility that I had no opportunity to be a child. My mother worked twelve-hour shifts. I looked after my sister, who was four years younger than me, and cared for my World War II disabled father. I was the caretaker, and my mother was the provider. I had no caretaker. I was tired when I grew up, and I did not want to care-take anymore. I really did not want children.

I wanted freedom and no responsibility. I was happy when a physician's opinion rendered I was unable to have children. Those words released me from worry. I could spend the rest of my life thinking about myself and doing what I wanted to do when I wanted to do it. I could be totally self-absorbed. I married, and the two of us, in the beginning, thought we were happy and fulfilled in our little world.

We built a weekend vacation home in the Great Smoky Mountains of Tennessee. The house was the size of our imaginings, big. Our house sat above a waterfall. The fourth floor had a collapsible glass wall that overlooked the falls. The water and the mountains were mesmerizing in their peace and solace. We were so happy to be out of the big city and rid of its freeways, crime, noise, congestion, and distractions. When our second home was completed, we found we could no longer return to the noise of the city. We sold everything and moved to the mountains permanently. We were young enough to begin again in a place where we would awaken to the birds and retire with the crickets. We began our second life in this pastoral setting with no caretaking and no responsibility except for each other.

One month after moving to those beautiful mountains, I became very ill. I vomited, lost my appetite, and had a menstrual cycle that would not end. I could not sleep, and yet, I could not get out of bed. I grew thin, and we grew concerned. I distrusted doctors for what I had seen them do to my father, so I refused to see one. I thought my sickness would pass, but it got worse. Finally, I went to see the doctor.

When I came out of the examining room, I was pale, scared, and filled with fear. I told my husband, "We are going to have a baby." He was stunned, and then, I saw his tears of joy. We were going to have a baby! I explained that my chances of a normal delivery were slim. I was very ill and very weak. We drove home silently; each lost in our own thoughts.

I was going to be a mother when I had never been a child. I was lost in my loss. I was being torn from my self-absorption and again having to care for a helpless human. The difference was that this human would grow in me and come from me. I longed for freedom. I longed for me.

We discussed abortion, and then we quit discussing abortion. We discussed the risk, and then we quit discussing the risk. We discussed my many women friends who had children and raised them in between a career and domestic responsibilities. Their husbands' careers, often considered the first priority, left these women at home struggling to keep the roles of wife, mother, and professional in balance. They were the ones who made the sacrifices for their families. I had made my sacrifices. I did not want more.

After much discussion, he agreed that we would be a team and we would raise this child together. We agreed to the things that I could not do, and he agreed to do them. As I had fed my father during the last years of his debilitating disease, he agreed to feed this child when the time came, as I could not feed another human with a spoon. He agreed that I would not be left behind to raise this child. He agreed we would all travel together no matter where our business took us. I was sad in the loss of what was my perception of freedom and again assuming responsibility when I thought responsibility for me was completed. I was afraid for I knew nothing about babies, and I had only seven months to learn.

We had this child after twenty-three hours of intense labor and a caesarian section, where the anesthesia did not take effect quickly and I felt the cut. I awakened to someone's tears falling on my face. He said, "We have a healthy baby boy." He was healthy, 9 pounds 14 ounces and 22" long. No wonder I could not push him out of my small frame. In later years, I would frequently accuse him of being so warm, comfortable, and secure in that uterine environment that he could not bear to enter the stark world of human reality.

I said, "Name him Dmitri, after my father." I fell into a deep sleep that took away my pain and redefined my freedom. Twenty-two months later, his brother Dakus was born by appointment. He was not a possibility, according to the doctor. There he was, arriving by C-section, once again. They took caution to drug me heavily. I resisted reentry into consciousness. They had to slap me to bring me back from where my drugged stupor had allowed me to wander. Now, I had two where I had wanted none.

I sit here and look back there, where I was once. My sons have taken me to places that I never knew existed and to places I could not go unless they took me. They had the keys to the locked doors of my childhood innocence. Amazingly, their world paralleled my world. They held my hand, allowing me to move at my own rhythm. As we grew together, those doors opened, and my life expanded. They guided my path with their innocence and their trust in my guardianship.

Their patience was infinite, and their love without conditions. Their trust was unshakable and their compassion simple. They loved me when I was energized and when I was weary. They loved me when I was just and when I was unjust. They loved me when I was reasonable and when I was unreasonable. They loved me, always.

I learned how to love through their love of me. I had not known this love before they came into my life. A child's love is like no other. It is not of this world. They bring the magic of love with them as they enter through us. Their love is pure. In their helplessness, they touch chords that we abandoned playing long ago when we lost our innocence. They remind us of those distant memories. If we have any trust or spirit left, they rekindle those dying embers, and we grow as they grow. We become children again with them. We experience the freedom that love brings. We experience surrender.

A self-absorbed life is one that is folded in upon its self. It has no light. Without light, we have no vision. The self-absorbed love we have to offer to others is an extension of our ego and our needs, hence no moment is fulfilled. Because the ego cannot be satisfied, there is never enough love from anyone. We move from one empty moment to another. We drift and search for purpose, never looking inward towards our own buried childhood purity.

It is our children who reintroduce us to innocence again. The time that their incorruptibility surrounds us is fleeting. Parents, whose lives are inundated with diversions, often undernourish this childhood innocence. In the clutter of this distracted family life, the sweet virtue of their children fades before it is recognized. We all suffer in this untimely loss of purity. Our children, who become like us, learn to live and survive in this distracted world. The embers of our own childhood clarity are slowly extinguished as our children grow towards the standards we set. We all lose.

With the birth of my sons, I lost my freedom of self-absorption and doing what I wanted to do when I wanted to do it. My guardianship of their innocence illuminated my path into another freedom. I relived with them my lost childhood and they helped to melt the frozen chambers of my heart.

They took my hand and showed me the Way. Their hands were so little for such a big job.

THE FIRST YEARS

2. THE FIRST YEARS

I was scared.

I never took a course in child rearing. Throughout all of my schooling, there was never a lesson on children and their care, family life, or marriage. I had the memories of my own childhood upon which to reflect, and they were less than satisfying. My sons and I were beginning a long journey together, and I had only a vague notion of the first steps in these first years.

I remember thinking how slowly children grow. It took so long for them to become adults. I had to fill all of the spaces in between. What would I do to occupy them? How would I prepare them for a world and a future that was unimaginable to me with the only constant being change? They would have to be educated toward those unknowns with a lot of guessing and no guarantees.

I felt overwhelmed. I began with the simple things of motherhood, things that I could successfully and easily accomplish. I bathed them, nourished them, and held them. I breast-fed them in a rocking chair, which I had placed in our bedroom in front of the TV. It was quiet up there on the second floor, where big windows opened into the treetops. They fed while I watched reruns of Star Trek. This helped the boredom of sitting there with nothing else to do. It was peaceful, and that was a good thing because I needed time to adjust to being a mother. I needed quiet moments with them. There were no interruptions in the mountains, only birds singing in the morning and crickets chirping in the evening. We began the process of getting to know each other, the caretaker and her wards.

The months slipped by quietly as I wove myself into motherhood. I made baby food from the vegetables in our garden. I educated myself on nutrition and early childhood brain development. I thought about the education of their young minds and where to begin. I watched them observe me. Their helplessness was so unexpected and something for which I was unprepared. They took everything I had in those early years. In return, their innocence rekindled the faded memory of my lost innocence, and we became equals in learning and loving.

There were times when they would reach up and touch my breast as they fed. Their hands were so little. We grew intimate. Intimacy requires vulnerability, and we were vulnerable in those years, me in the role of a lifetime and them wide-eyed and helpless. There they were with clean, clear, uncluttered minds. There I was with a lifetime of baggage, some wisdom, and lots of knowledge that was mostly useless. What a trio we made!

They made me think. I thought about how much I was learning about love. I thought about how this love from these two small beings was not like any love I had experienced. I thought about the innocence we bring into the world when we first arrive. I wondered how it left us as we grew. I wanted to keep it for them as long as I could. The day we lose our innocence goes unnoticed. It is stolen without a sound.

I thought back upon my own childhood and those early years of my life. I believe as parents we all go back in our memories, so we may try and recall the outstanding moments of how we were raised. We draw upon those childhood experiences, so we may duplicate the best ones in rearing our own children. I tried to remember my parents and recall what role they played in my child rearing. I wanted to avoid the haphazard, unintentional errors in judgment that influenced my life in unproductive directions. I wanted to be sure that my family baggage would not be bequeathed to my sons.

My father was the first man I ever knew. He was the first man I ever loved. He was the first man who made me feel important, and he was the first man who disappointed me. I hardly remember him. I never really knew him after the age of six. At the age of eight, I became his caretaker, and his light began to diminish. His unexpected illness slowly debilitated him during our lives together. As the years passed, my memories of him dimmed until a time came when I could hardly recall his being my father. He was unable to perform that function for me nearly all of my life. I did not know what it was like to have a father in the traditional sense. It was not his fault, but it did hurt with a pain that I could not explain to anyone, so I lived with it in silence, all of my life.

I was a World War II baby. Many of our fathers were gone in our early lives. I remember seeing my father for the first time. He was sitting at the kitchen table with my mother. He was in his army uniform and had just arrived from being discharged from the Army. I was supposed to be in bed, but I was hiding around the corner, taking a peek at this man. There he was, and I had no feelings other than curiosity in seeing him for the first time. I do remember how beautiful they looked together. I will never be able to erase that image from my mind, and I conjure it up occasionally, so I may remember him from the first time.

He was tall and handsome in his uniform. I saw him smile at her. He had a beautiful smile. His eyes lit up when he spoke to her. They were seeing each other for the first time in a long time. They were strangers then, so was I to him.

I don't remember when he saw me for the first time or how he felt. I have often wondered if he was pleased or disappointed. I guess I will never know, because in all the years I took care of him, I never asked. I don't ever remember him telling me that he loved me or that I was beautiful or smart. I did not expect it, because our roles were reversed. I lived without it, not knowing that it was missing. I don't know if I loved him like other daughters love their fathers. He was someone I had to take care of, and we never seemed to get beyond that. My mother worked long shifts; he depended upon me, and I responded. We never knew that we had missed something in not loving each other as fathers do daughters and daughters do fathers. We did not know that our lives would be forever impacted by that loss.

I remember some of the times before he became ill. I would sit at the window and wait for him to come home from work. I only knew him a year then, but he entranced me. He always came home at 5:30, and we ate dinner at six. I remember that the Good Humor Man came through our neighborhood in his white ice cream truck at seven. The Good Humor Man was the second most important man in my life then. He delivered great, joyful squeals with his bells, and he always fulfilled my expectations. The entire neighborhood waited for the Good Humor Man every night after dinner. All of us rushed out of our project housing in the mad dash to be the first to order from him. We pushed and shoved, so we could get our favorite flavors. The Good Humor Man never disappointed me. Those were my happiest days of great anticipation and joy, my dad and the Good Humor Man.

As soon as I heard his bells, my father would give me a nickel to buy my ice cream, which was my reward for eating everything on my plate. I always bought Dreamcicles. Sometimes my father would sit outside with me as I slowly licked the orange ice and inside cream. I thought if I ate it slowly it would last longer. We would talk. That is one of my few memories of him in the time when I was his "daughter". It is the thing that makes me feel he loved me then. I never saw the Good Humor Man after we moved to Miami for my father's health. I often asked my father in those days, "Whatever happened to the Good Humor Man?"

I spent my early youth helping my father navigate through the unknown and unexpected places in his life, as his disability with Multiple Sclerosis engulfed him. Our adjustments were daily and often had to be creative in their solutions to serious problems. If he fell, I had to help him up. I was small, so we had to work it out together. We shared a lot of sorrow. His eyes apologized if he dropped a glass or spilled the milk. He spent those early years embarrassed by his disability and his inabilities.

We spent a lot of our time alone, together. We didn't talk much. We observed each other. We sat in the same rooms with our own thoughts. He taught me how to play chess and let me win sometimes. He taught me the multiplication tables when I was failing math. He wanted me to succeed. He taught me how to dance. He saw my rhythm and showed me his. He came in and out of these small moments of my life. That is how I grew up with my father.

I was glad when my time came to go away to a university. It meant that I would be free from responsibility for the first time in my life. There was no caretaking, no meals to prepare and no cleanup. It was just me and no one else. I remember being a lost soul with all of that freedom. I was like a fish out of water. I did not understand balance. I did too much, or I did too little. I helped when it wasn't wanted, or I didn't ask for help when it was expected. I misjudged and misinterpreted the simplest actions often ending most encounters in confusion and disarray in those early days of freedom with no responsibility.

As my father was not there for me because of his disabilities and painful wheelchair life, I did not know what emotional support was, so I did not expect it. I only knew to give. I had no other expectations. My early relationships were dismal encounters.

I did not know how to ask for the simplest of things, because I could not ask my father for the simplest of things. He was physically unable to give. I learned how to do for myself. I was lonely in my self-sufficient world, but that is not what I called it. I was afraid of that word "lonely". It was a word that I could hardly speak. I called my condition "independent", which made me feel as if I were in control of my hapless self. I kept the truth of my needy nature buried deep within the frozen chambers of my heart. It was impossible to explore those chambers, for I did not know they were there. I lived my life in those early years as if I were like everyone else, because I thought I was then.

I think of my father and his strength, his patience and his wisdom. I think of the love he had for me and his awkward way of expressing it. He told me things that as a child I could not understand or comprehend. He stored his secrets in my memory, and much later in my life, they came forth to save me from the indignities that others accept as normal. He gave me his humor and his easy laughter. He loaned me his smile for this lifetime. But most importantly of all, he demonstrated to me on a daily basis how to live life with strength and compassion, how to overcome obstacles, and how to move forward. When I look back, I am always amazed at how adversity builds character and strength. I thought about that as I thought about my sons and wondered if it would be possible to build these traits without adversity?

I was with him the night he died spiritually. I sat at the foot of his bed; it was late in the evening. He had been sleeping all day, nearly unconscious. I was reading when he sat up; he looked at the ceiling and smiled that beautiful smile I see in my memory of him. I asked, "Daddy, what are you looking at?" He did not respond. He lay back down and never spoke again. I knew then that he would not be back, for he had seen where he was going.

I loved him. I hope he knew it. His body died four days later.

My mother was a child who had a child, and we seemed to grow up together. She was a strict disciplinarian who demanded good grades in school and good behavior. I can barely remember the early years when she was just a mother who cooked and took care of family life. I was too young and only have brief glimpses into those memories. My strongest recollections now are of her working twelve hour shifts, struggling to pay bills, feed the family and keep us all together. She had no one to turn to for assistance, and so she turned to me to assume the household responsibilities at an early age. I became the one in charge when she was gone. She would talk to me as if I were an adult, and we shared many hard times together. I have always believed that children meet their parents' expectations, and I did meet hers. She had no other options, and as a result, my childhood ended early. The adult in me emerged as family responsibilities grew beyond her control. I became her "girlfriend" as we devised ways to pay for the necessities of life.

The insecurities of never having enough drew us into a collaboration that was unbalanced for a mother-daughter relationship. Many of the serious life situations that confronted us in my early childhood created within me a tension that never fully disappeared even until this day. I spent most of my life in fear: fear of no money, fear of no food, fear of no shelter, fear of things as a child that only adults experience. These fears established roots that created heavy baggage for me to carry into my adult life. I learned to quietly bury these fears so as not to burden my mother whose life seemed overwhelming to me. She was the force that kept life going, and in my young mind she could not be disturbed with my small problems, for hers seemed so great from my perspective. I know that she felt guilty about my early life and the hardships that were thrust upon me. Even though this is what gave me the strength I would need to survive the yet unimaginable hardships I would face in my life, I often wonder what life would have been like for me if I had had her emotional support.

On those misty days when I look out into the mountains, I remember her laughter in the face of the most ominous events. She would take life-threatening situations, and as I quivered in fear, her humor would splash over me. She would turn my tears into laughter, and we would begin again to keep our family afloat in our little boat.

26

When we moved to Miami, she applied for a job working as a secretary. When she couldn't make enough money to support us, she became a waitress. In those days, tips went unreported to the IRS. One day, there was a knock at the door. She was getting dressed for the night shift. I opened the door, and there stood two IRS agents in dark suits. I was only nine then. They came in, and they had a conversation with her that I cannot recall. I do remember this most vivid event. They threatened to arrest her. The small light in my soul flickered as I hid in the hallway. There was my father in a wheelchair, my small sister in another room. If she left, how would I support them? She looked at me sternly, and I knew to stay back. I was always so afraid in those days. I guess it was because I always felt so helpless.

She stood to her full 5' 2" height and said, "I need a place to rest from this hard life. You take care of my disabled husband and my two small children. I am tired, and it would be nice to be taken care of for a while." They turned ashen. They were shocked. They did not terrify her. I watched in amazement at how they quickly made their compromise with her and worked out a payment plan.

They left, and she turned this ominous event into something funny. We laughed in between my tears, and she brought me back out of fear once again. She knew the toll this role was taking on me, but there were no options. In an attempt to comfort me she said, "Fear no man. Fear only the wrath of God. No man has power over you unless you give him that power." I will always remember her standing in our small living room looking up at those tall men. She impacted them. Later, one of them called and came by to see how we were managing with their payment plan. She had a way with people that showed in how they responded to her.

Her uncanny, God-given, intuitive sense into people sheltered us from uncertainty. When it counted, she was ferocious, and her ferocity was the only security I had in my childhood. She was the only physical demonstration of power that I observed. She was always teaching me in the time she was not sleeping or working. She used to say, "It's the little people who will help you in time of trouble, not the big shots. The big shots get to where they are going by stepping on the little people. Stay close to the little people. They will be there for you."

She was generous with her time; for that was the only wealth she would ever have in her lifetime. I remember many mornings, waking up for school to find her cooking pancakes for a bar hooker who was down on her luck or a hapless friend who was in a jam and needed comfort. Her heart was made of gold, and I am sure that there were many times she wished she could have pawned it.

She detested prejudice, and hence our home was open to anyone who needed help. This amazed me, for we needed help more than some of those who came to our kitchen for pancakes and coffee. She knew I disapproved and that I was growing miserly for fear of going hungry. She would tell me when she saw me counting eggs, "Never take the great risk of eliminating someone from your life who might change its course or increase its depth!" She would utter these sentiments with great passion throughout my growing up with her. I finally stopped counting eggs.

She changed jobs. The heavy food trays were grinding her down. She became a bartender. She wore boots to work and came home as I was getting up for school. I would help pull her boots off. They were laden with bills and change. I would put the money on her bedside table and take fifty cents for my sister and me for school lunch. She fell asleep exhausted as I made breakfast, dressed my sister, and helped my father. She would tell me, "Someday these quarters will put you through college." They did. We were a team!

She always felt I didn't know enough. Once she told me how sad it made her that my father was unable to teach me the ways of men. We sat down, and she poured herself a drink. She loved her scotch. She had some time to talk to me, but it had to be fast. She said, "Always remember that men are basically selfish and that they only think of three things; Sex, Money and Power and in that order." She went on to say, "Believe only what you see, never what you hear!" It was this whispered wisdom in those fearful years that made no sense to me at the time, but upon which I drew as an adult in my times of trouble. All of our brief conversations and her wisdom came back to me, eventually.

She was worried that I was approaching the dating age, and my sequestered life of care taking had left a gap in my understanding of men. I think that she wanted to keep me unpregnant. We talked further but it was the last statement that day that I carried with me into my adult life, "You are innocent and terribly naïve, and I regret that. But I have a feeling that this will protect you from harm. People see it, and no one shoots a doe in an open field."

One late night I found my mother crying quietly in the kitchen, the place where so many souls had eaten. She asked me to sit down; she had to talk, and I was her girlfriend. My father had long ago moved into his own bedroom because of his terrible illness. She had fallen in love with a man who offered an ultimatum and a choice. He offered her a nursing home for my father, private boarding schools for her daughters, and a life free at last from insecurity and fear. She was crying because she could not leave my father, a man whom she ceased to love in that way. She cried because my sister and I would never have the private education and the fine dresses. She cried that she could not walk away from us. She cried for the loss of the man she loved. I cried, because I loved her and I knew I could not help her. She talked until 5:00 AM, and then she stopped crying. I made coffee, and we began again to talk in low tones.

She said very softly, "Remember what I am going to tell you now. Never betray your commitments. We will survive, and you will have the best I can offer. We cannot live without your father, he depends on our protection. If I left him, who would love and take care of him like we do?"

We knew no one would love or take care of him like we did. We knew his heart would break if he were shunted off to a nursing home and made to live among strangers. What would become of this proud man's dignity? We knew the betrayal of trust would invade every aspect of our lives as our responsibilities towards husband and father were traded in for comfort and splendor. He would not survive. The price was too expensive, and we could not afford the goods. I remember saying to her, "It is you who taught me that a life without honor is no life at all." I told her that we didn't need what she thought we needed and we looked at each other in that very still moment knowing that life was not going to get any easier and we would struggle.

She went into my father's room and looked at him sleeping in his bed. Tears flowed from her eyes. She had made the most important unselfish decision of her life. It caused her great pain and great loss. She went on, and we survived. My sister and I went to college, and both of us graduated. We both left home, and she was alone with her pain and my father. She and I never discussed that night again. We acted as if it never happened. She continued to laugh at life's obstacles, and she took care of my father until the day he died.

She never remarried. She never fell in love again. She moved and bought a small home where she lived alone. She surrounded herself with books and read voraciously.

My Mother died on Sunday, January 23, 2000. They say they found her by the phone. She was my last best friend. She was the last person I loved from my past. I miss her terribly. I miss her wisdom and the truths she gave me about the long journey into my life. We spent that last New Year's Eve on the phone together. We discussed my failed marriage. She said, "I am so worried that you are still so innocent and naïve when it comes to men, but that may work in your favor because no one shoots a doe in an open field." We laughed because I had not changed, and it was still her worry.

Four feet of fresh snow fell in the mountains that Saturday night. She died on Sunday. I was snowbound and alone in those beautiful Tennessee Mountains. I was trapped and could not find a way out to say good-by. I will have to say it here. The pain is still so great. I cannot think of her as a memory.

The last time she saw my sons the three of them drove off into the mountains together. They were ten and twelve. She decided they needed to get to know each other better. She talked about "Yatze", a game she enjoyed playing with some friends. She told them some of her secrets, which they kept secret. She bought them gifts and splurged her grandmother's love and pride upon them. She talked and talked and talked. They were going to bed that night, and I asked how their day went. They said, "Bubby sure does talk a lot."

I responded, "She always had a lot to say and very little time in which to say it. Her life was lived between sleep and work. She had very little time, but the time she did have was always spent in preparing me for life."

Dakus said, "Do you know what she told us Mom?"

"What?"

"When we told her that she sure did talk a lot, she said, 'Silence is for corpses.'"

THE PATH

3. THE PATH

Our sons would have a very different life from mine.

I would craft and weave a childhood of opportunity, energy, and love around them. I would focus on being the kind of mother I did not have, on securing the kind of home I did not have, and on creating a stable emotional environment that I did not have, so we could foster an intellectual climate of challenge and diversity within our family. I had so much to learn and so little time in which to learn it. I knew nothing about children, and I had no resource from which to draw upon. I had only distant memories and some sparse wisdom that was whispered to me in my early childhood years.

I had lived with fear all of my life, and I knew its limitations. It was something I had to conquer before my sons came into their awareness. How tragic it would be for me to perpetuate a history of turmoil in their innocent lives. I had to lift myself out of the history of my past and visualize a future that could only be imagined. Each day had to be thoughtfully considered. I knew there would be times I would fall back, but I could not afford to stay there long. How unjust it would be to shade these fragile souls who were looking for light.

I sat up late one evening, looking at the stars from our living room deck. I was embarking upon a long journey that would end only when I ended. I thought about the fragility of life as it starts its journey. My memory flooded with the thought of the newly hatched turtles that dash from the beach to reach the ocean's waters and the many predators they faced when reaching their home in the sea. I wondered how many succeeded.

It came to me that life was not an accident but a gift. It had to be opened carefully, and a faith in the guidance of something higher would lead me to the unfolding of myself, so that in my understanding I would bring understanding. We can only deliver what we understand. I had to change myself before I could mold another. We three were beginning a long journey together, and they came so I could finally begin mine. At that star struck moment, a memory from my early childhood repeated itself to me,

> *"The light of the body is the eye:*
> *if therefore thine eye be single, thy*
> *whole body shall be full of light.*
>
> *But if thine eye be evil, thy whole*
> *body shall be full of darkness. If*
> *therefore the light that is in thee be*
> *darkness, how great is that darkness!"*

Matthew Chapter 6. 22, 23.

So it was here that we would begin, in the light, not the darkness. We would learn together, the caretaker and her wards. I would attempt to leave fear behind me. I would create the way for us by changing the things I could change within myself and being aware of the things I could not change. The few primitive remnants from the unchangeable distant past would not cloud the light in our journey. We would build emotional support with a strong foundation of love. We would be responsible for ourselves, mother, father, and sons. We would be parents first and their friends later. We would teach, share, laugh, and cry together. We would have a vision for their future and open avenues for them to explore. We would create the threads from which our tapestry would be woven each day, one day at a time. There would be moments when clouds would gather, but we would bathe mostly in the sun light. There would always be big arms and warm hearts at the end of the day. We would build character and strength without tribulation. We would live together in harmony, so that each day could be a memory. There would always be food, shelter, and love.

I knew there would be hard times, good times, sad times, and happy times. What is life without tests? No test should be experienced without strong emotional support, for it is the tests that let us know who we are. We would all grow in the tests that life would bring to our family and we would all expand in our knowledge of each other and ourselves. At the end of the journey, we would have two sons who would make a difference in the lives of the people they touched, and they would then begin another generation. Their vision would be so much greater than mine, for they would come from a life of light.

My mother used to tell me in some of our quiet moments together, "It is the responsibility of each generation to improve the next."

THE LIGHT

4. THE LIGHT

Standing here now and looking back at the view, I see clearly the light that flowed into each decision. It was not so apparent then. There were many times I acted on instinct with no logic to support my decisions. Often, I did not know the path to take. I was inexperienced and had to rely on my past life encounters and my intuition.

I noticed how I drew closer to Divine Guidance and Faith. I noticed how I prayed in silence, a lot. My spirituality grew as they grew. I put my trust in something I could not see or hear. I could only feel it. That feeling stayed with me, and it was not something I could talk about. I just acknowledged it and went on with my decisions, hoping these intuitive feelings would open opportunities for creative, intellectual expansion for these two small souls.

My two sons took hold of me, and raising them well became the most important role in my life. I could not explain it even to myself. I marveled at their innocence. It captivated me. I had never experienced anything like it before. My own innocence was buried before I became a child, and through them, I was able to peek into that unwritten chapter in my life. Their smiles and eyes radiated awestruck wonder, and it mesmerized me. Just beneath this innocence were waters whose depths were too deep for me to see. I knew that we would swim together in the shallows until we grew comfortable, and, quietly in these mountains, we would begin our journey into those depths.

I began looking at babies everywhere I went. I saw the same wonder in those infant eyes, the same innocence, and the same smiles. I noticed that babies smiled a lot. I believe those smiles are worn to please and to express the joy of being. They must please so they are protected, and joy is difficult to hide. My world was expanding; everything was changing.

The solitude of the mountains became our cocoon as we grew up together. I saw the wonders of childhood in their first-time experiences: the first time they saw snow, the first time they dipped their small hands in a bucket of paint and withdrew them in color, the first time they robbed bee hives for their honey, the first time they saw me cry. They touched me in spaces where no one had before. Being their mother was a profound and loved-filled experience, a gift not an accident.

I wanted them to have all of the things that I thought I never had. Most importantly, I wanted them to be surrounded with love and hope. I wanted their lives filled with light and for each day to be important. I wanted them to have memories of family tradition, warmth, challenges, emotional support, and intellectual stimulation. I wanted those memories to sustain them in the storms that are inevitable in all our lives. That is where they would draw their strength, just as I drew mine from the whisperings of my father and mother. I knew they would observe their father and mother, and what they saw is what they would believe. Raising children is a thoughtful undertaking.

There was no time to waste, for there was much to learn before they went away. They had to be educated, knowing that the only certainty was uncertainty. They needed options in a world that changed daily. It was no longer possible to adopt one vocation and expect personal and professional success indefinitely. There were too many variables that could significantly impact a single vision life. It was essential to develop multiple visions and expose them to many paths. They needed to know how to do many things, so they would face as few unknowns as possible. It is the unknown that terrorizes us. The fear of that unknown blinds us from seeing an array of solutions to our problems. As we educate towards multiplicity, enlightenment, and understanding, we experience fewer unknowns. The narrow path of success then becomes a boulevard.

I knew that the early years, birth to six, were the most important years of brain and skill development. The positive reinforcement of their childhood wonder and their creative self-expression would mold their character and confidence. I needed to be attentive as these delicate, early years evolved. Much to my surprise, the experiences that brought light dancing in their toddler eyes involved color, music, small animals, nature, and miniscule things they would pick up and study for what seemed an endless time.

This should not have surprised me for it is art that enhances creative self-expression and our appreciation of beauty. It is the universal language of music that plays with our emotions. Music makes us "one" with many strangers at a concert or "one" within the solitude of the rooms in which we live. It is small animals that teach us the value of patience, caretaking and unconditional love. It is the power and diversity of nature that demonstrates consistency and change. It is the miniscule things we study along the way that multiply our questions. Every day they were showing me the way. All I had to do was observe them and listen.

I began to summon my educational skills from my early years as a teacher. I had taught in the public school system for six years when I completed college. I was disappointed with my results. My ideas were not readily received. Many of them were rejected. Like many new teachers who leave the universities, I was filled with enthusiasm and my desire to make things better through change with my newly acquired teaching certificate. They did not tell me in my graduate courses that no one wanted change and that things were just fine as they were. We were sent out into a system that was highly structured, filled with administrative tasks, and prepared to justify the rejection of ideas that were "unconventional".

I was given the state-approved textbooks, thirty desks with thirty students, a blackboard, and lots of chalk. I was assigned five classes, one teacher's rest period, a lunch break, and after-school sponsorship of a school club. There were no other teaching aids during this incredible time when Marshall McLuhan was publishing, "The Medium is the Message". There were no visual aids during this time when all of my students were seriously transitioning into the age of multimedia sensory perception, psychedelic musical mystery tours, occult readings, pot, and questions – many, many questions.

I remember standing at the front of those classes while they sat at their thirty desks, all in neat rows. I remember saying, "Open your books to page 167, take out your homework, and let's review your questions". They looked so bored. I did not have time to change the boredom. I had to complete the state-approved textbooks by the end of the year, so they could pass their exams. I, too, was bored. What I was teaching seemed hardly relevant to the times in which these children lived. I was the lowest of the low, a young classroom teacher with no seniority or power. I did what I was told for as long as I could take it, and then, one day, six years later, I left the system and never went back. I could not flourish in irrelevancy.

It was near the end of this first year that I was sent a printed note by one of my college professors. It was to change my perspective forever on many things in my life. It read:

"I have taught in high school for ten years. During that time I have given assignments, among others, to a murderer, an evangelist, a pugilist, a thief and an imbecile.

The Murderer was a quiet little boy who sat on the front seat and regarded me with pale blue eyes; the evangelist, easily the most popular boy in the school, had the lead in the junior play; the pugilist lounged by the window and let loose at intervals a raucous laugh that startled even the geraniums; the thief was a gay hearted Lothario with a song on his lips; and the imbecile, a soft spoken little animal seeking the shadows.

The murderer awaits death in the state penitentiary; the evangelist has lain a year now in the village churchyard; the pugilist lost an eye in a brawl in Hong Kong; the thief, by standing on tiptoe, can see the windows of my room from the county jail; and the once gentle eyed little moron beats his head against a padded wall in the state asylum.

All of these pupils once sat in my room, sat and looked at me gravely across worn brown desks. I must have been a great help to those pupils I taught them the rhyming scheme of the Elizabethan sonnet and how to diagram a complex sentence."

Anonymous

Remembering all of my professional teaching frustrations, I resolved as a mother to spare our sons from the boredom of standardized educational convention and mediocrity. I would follow my instinct, good sense, and intuition in creating an educational path upon which our sons would travel. My life experiences and "Mom" power in the home school we were about to begin, would develop an educational lifestyle that was creative and intellectually challenging. Our young sons would lead, and I would follow. Whenever they seriously changed their interests, their early childhood education would add these new interests to their curriculum. This would be an attempt to enlighten, to illuminate, and to inspire. They were the teachers, and I was the student. It was here we began our journey into the unknown with only the tools of my firm belief in Divine Guidance, my Faith and intuition, their innocence and my determination to spare their lives from irrelevancy and boredom.

It was my conspiracy, and their father was my collaborator. He supported our little school. He helped and assisted in the background. He helped me to laugh when I entered troubled waters. He was accustomed to my unconventional beliefs and my creative lifestyle. I will always love and appreciate him for his utter belief in me. We never wavered. We were a loving team.

We began home schooling when Dmitri was three and Dakus was one and a half. We started with simple things to test their curiosity and spirit. As their curiosity grew beyond us, we moved the school into our two-car garage. We called ourselves, "The Children's School". Our school motto was, "If we can think it, we will do it". Our first school mascot was a crippled groundhog, who came out of the woods one day dragging his undeveloped hind legs. We fed him and named him Blue, for the color of the sky. Our school garage doors were opened in pretty weather and many wood animals would come by to eat and drink the water we left out, take a look inside, and return to the woods. Our school song was whatever anyone sang the loudest. For a time we were a little partial to "Itsy, Bitsy, Spider".

After a while, we hired a certified teacher, and I worked with her to develop a curriculum based upon reading, writing, arithmetic and all of the curiosities that four, five, and six-year-olds become intrigued with as they grow. Soon after, we hired special consultants from the wider community of the University of Tennessee and Oak Ridge, where the national laboratories are located. There existed a wealth of graduate students and retired PhD's available for some of our special school projects. The Children's School began at 8:00 am and ended at 4:00 pm. but it was always in session. It did not end when our teacher, Nancy, and the consultants went home at the end of the day. Education is not a process that begins at 8:00 am and ends at 4:00 pm. Learning continues as long as curiosity persists.

Through this extraordinary process of learning, I discovered my internal universe as they explored their external universe. We truly did grow up together. Parenting is a profound experience. It is intimate, intuitive, and faithful. It is a lifelong commitment. It is filled with small stories every day. It makes a difference to the world how we fulfill the commitment of parenting. If we do it well, the world benefits. If we do it poorly, the world suffers. It is as simple as that.

We learned many lessons along the way. Extraordinary insights lay buried in ordinary events. We unearthed treasures with hard work and open minds. Many times what we dug up was not what we expected. Their little minds with their many revelations seriously changed my inner universe. "The Child is father of the Man…"

Come with me, and I will take you on a journey, which began 30 years ago and has not yet ended. I will share with you some little stories of love, innocence, and light. Come and be a part of this experience that is written in my memory. Come see how motherhood changed every preconceived notion of how I defined myself. Come into these pages and read where I began my life so many years after I thought I had lived it.

"The light of the body is the eye:
if therefore thine eye be single, thy
whole body shall be full of light."

THE SLED

5. THE SLED

It had snowed through the night in our Tennessee Mountains. There was a foot of pure white fluff on the ground when we awakened that morning. Dmitri had never seen snow before. He had just reached the age of awareness of his external surroundings. His stunned amazement and curiosity captivated me. I had forgotten what it was like to see something for the first time. I could not recall that feeling of wonder, excitement, and enormous curiosity. I watched him as he looked out through the window at the white landscape. I hoped that he would help me to see what he saw as we looked together through the glass.

His bright blue eyes made me feel so childlike again. I became enraptured with the thought of showing him the snow and experiencing it with him. I dressed him in two pairs of pants, a woolen cap, my woolen scarf, his little coat, gloves and boots. We walked outside together. He picked up the snow and studied it for a bit. He tasted it, and then, he jumped from the step into this fluff. It settled up past his little knees.

We had a steep driveway at the time, which was the perfect place for a sled ride. I had no sled, so I tried to describe to him what a sled was and how it worked. He looked up at me with his bright eyes and rosy cheeks and innocently said, "Make a sled." To children anything is possible.

We found a large, thick cardboard box in the garage. We put several plastic garbage bags inside of it to make it waterproof and waxed the bottom of it with an old candle. We punched two holes in the front and found some old string I had saved. We knotted the string and tied it through the holes. The string became a handle and *we* had a sled.

We looked at each other with glee and excitement as we entered into our adventure. We had the greatest sled on the planet! Dmitri laughed and shouted as I lifted him into the sled. His eyes sparkled, and he looked so healthy. I remember standing there at that moment in time with the string in my hand looking at him in the sled. He was so trusting and pure in his love for me. He knew that this was going to be a good time, and I knew that he would forever love the snow.

I looked down the steep driveway and thanked God that he had the wisdom to give us babies when we were young enough to pull sleds down steep driveways and back again. We went sliding through the snow at what I shouted out to be "the speed of light". The sled would tumble over with snow flying in all directions. Dmitri would roll out screaming, and we would walk back up to the top again. He held my hand, so I wouldn't fall.

After a while, he wanted to pull me down the driveway. I told him he was too little to pull a sled with such a big person in it. He said that he would "push" the sled. He was determined that I go at "the speed of light", so I could have fun too. I cautiously climbed into the sled. My legs hung out over the sides. I just fit to his great satisfaction. He pushed. I didn't budge, so I began to row with my arms. We got to the incline, he pushed as hard as he could, and the sled suddenly took off. Down I went in a rush. He fell into the snow at the top of our steep driveway, having pushed the sled as hard as he could.

Half way down the driveway, the out-of-control sled toppled over, and I was thrown into the snow. He came running after me. I was covered in snow. I looked up from the snow, and he was standing over me. I saw fear and tears in those beautiful blue eyes. He feverishly began to brush me off. He said, "I love you, Mommy, you all right? I push too hard."

I was stunned by his two-year-old love for me. I cannot forget the memory of his eyes. I will never forget the sound of his voice. I saw his deep, innocent, and very pure love for me at that moment. My life meant so much to him. In this small, seemingly insignificant cardboard sled snow event, he defined my importance and value. I grabbed him, and pulled him down into the snow with me. We rolled, laughed, hugged, and kissed. His worry left and his big love returned to its safe haven. He was reassured that I was fine, and he had done nothing wrong. We learned the right lessons that snow-covered day.

The light began to leave as the day grew shorter. We gathered up our stuff, which littered the snow. He took my hand and said, "I help you home. We had fun." I could not have made it up the road without him.

We bathed in a hot tub with lots of bubbles. We sat together in front of the fire in our rocking chair and talked about the sled and how clever we were. He put his arms around me, laid his head on my shoulder, and I hummed a lullaby. We both drifted off into our own thoughts. I will never know his, but mine were profound. I had experienced my son's love; a kind I never knew existed. His big love gave me purpose. It cleared a path to a road that eventually became our highway of carefully-considered decisions.

That day he led me caringly into motherhood and the depth of the extraordinary adventure of child rearing. He demonstrated the simple clarity of love, a concept that had been blurred in my early life. My love in my childhood days was filled with fear of loss. His love was filled with my welfare. There were two mothers, his and mine. Mine was my only security out of fear and helplessness. His was a part of his larger world.

I looked at him differently after that incident. He reaffirmed my faith and the importance of my intuition of how our sons should be raised. In that simple incident, I peeked into the world of how a child loves his mother. We both peeked into something for the first time that day.

His love opened doors in my heart that had closed so long ago. I was different the next morning. I was lighter. He helped to save me from mediocrity in the most important commitment I ever made.

They come to us to keep the memory of love alive and to remind us that there is no love purer than the love of a child. They are our teachers. We are their caretakers.

HIDE AND SEEK

6. HIDE AND SEEK

It seems so long ago now that I look back on it, their little game of Hide and Seek. The memory, however, is so vivid and colorful. My sons taught me so many lessons about life as we grew up together.

I was working in my home office. It was raining outside. My two children, one five and the other three, had nothing to do. I remember typing as one child came hurriedly through the front door and slipped into the coat closet. He said, "Mom, don't tell Dakus where I am."

I said, "OK", and then I began to type again.

In came Dakus, "Mom, where is Dmitri?"

"I don't know."

"I have to do a pooh-pooh."

"Good, go use the bathroom, turn the light on and, Dakus, don't forget to pull your pants down."

"Dakus, where am I?"

Dmitri, from his well-hidden place in the closet, was anxious for his brother to get on with the quest.

"Dmitri, where are you?"

I glanced at Dakus, and there he stood with his pants half down.

"Come find me, Dakus."

"But, I don't know where you are!"

"Look for me Dakus."

Dmitri failed to realize that every time he raised his voice to encourage Dakus to find him, he slowly gave himself away.

Dakus had a gleeful look on his face as he held his pants up with one hand. "I know where you are!"

"Come find me," Dmitri pleaded.

Dakus inched closer to where the voice was loudest.

"I found you! I found you in the closet!"

Dakus screamed jubilantly as he pulled the door open.

"You found me Dakus!" (So happy that he was found and didn't have to stay hidden much longer.) "Now I'll hide again, and you come find me."

"I have to do a pooh-pooh first."

"Turn the light on, and, Dakus don't forget to pull your pants down."

"Mooooom, I know!"

Dmitri heaves a sigh of relief and satisfaction. He hid and was found by the very person that he wanted to discover him. It never occurred to him that he gave himself away. It only mattered that he was found. Dakus, thrilled that he found Dmitri, felt successful and warmed by his brother's delight at having been found by him.

It was a simple, honest game. It never got too hard to play. There was lots of laughter and shrieking glee. It was an, "I'll hide and you find me game and if I am lost too long I'll help you with little clues so we can have some more fun finding each other again."

As they grew up, I wondered if they would be as hard to find as those who make us search without a clue. There are some who hide so well they are never found and blame us for our stumbling around. I wish we could be children all our lives.

THE ICE STORM

7. THE ICE STORM

The rain came first. It fell all day, and then, the temperature began to drop. The rain in the trees and on the ground turned to sheets of ice. As the rain continued falling, it gradually turned to snow. The snow fell all night. We awakened suddenly in the dark to loud, thunderous, ear-shattering noises as trees split in half, ice-laden limbs broke, and roots gave way under the drenched soil. Trees began falling all around us. It was terrifying. We knew as the trees went down, passage in and out of our mountain community would be blocked. No one had predicted this storm. We were all totally unprepared for its ferocity.

By morning, several hundred fallen trees littered our long driveway leading through the woods to our house. Hundreds of trees fell across the roads coming into our mountain community. As trees came down they took with them power poles and phone lines. Those fallen poles and lines removed all of the comforts that make winter bearable. We had no heat, no water from our wells, which depended on power, and no light. Our neighbors, spread out over 1200 acres, were unreachable. We had no way of helping each other. Because the communities in the valley had a substantial population and considerable tourism, they became the power company's priority. Our small mountain community was isolated. We were removed from the mainstream and on our own until help arrived. The scene from our kitchen window was catastrophic. It had the surreal look of a war zone, bombed out and devastated.

Imagine impassable roads, no television, no radio, no phones, and no outside communication with anyone. Imagine below freezing temperatures for more than ten days without heat, water, and light. Imagine no people, just silence, except for the sound of trees dropping under the weight of ice and snow. Imagine being trapped with no way out and all roads blocked by fallen trees. Imagine trying to keep animals alive and fed in below freezing temperatures. Imagine keeping our family fed by cooking in an open fire. Imagine food supplies dwindling each day and boiling lake water for our drinking needs.

As dismal as I perceived the situation to be, my young sons perceived the opposite. As I sunk into despair, they rose to a state of excitement and adventure. They had been studying the American Indians in our school, and they reminded me, "Mom, this is like camping out in the woods just like the Indians." I was not interested. I was inconvenienced.

No baths, oh what a wondrous way to begin each day for two little boys. They would dress in their warm, insulated hunting clothes, put their boots on, and rush outside to play in the snow, do some shoveling, help the animals, and haul wood, so I could keep the fires burning. They ate their breakfast of burnt bacon and over-cooked eggs with gusto and thanked me for the good job I was doing. They were in charge of feeding the chickens, turkeys, peacocks, and guinea hens. I was in charge of the two dogs and several cats. Their father was in charge of chopping wood and digging holes in the ice on the lake, so we could have water. As the fox moved in at night to kill our birds, the boys made a count each morning and totaled our losses. They were responsible for burials with their father. Each grave had a marker, which they made. A prayer was said, which was short. They would tell me how they were "toughing up" like the Indians and the pioneers. They were jovial and happy to help out in any way they could. They wanted to be men.

Three freezing days passed and no word from anyone. We were all sleeping in the "big" bed with our clothes on in order to stay warm. They loved it, camping out with Mom and Dad. I was falling deeper and deeper into a state of despair. There was no communication from anyone, no word of the state of the community from any source. I never felt more isolated and forgotten. The snow remained, and the temperatures stayed the same. There was no relief from the unbearable nothingness. I began to lose my temper, to shout at them, to criticize, and to be generally unkind and selfish. They took it all in and remained cheerful. They watched me change as each agonizing day dragged on endlessly.

The fourth day passed. We were dirty and cold. Our meals were tasteless and over-cooked. I was having a hard time getting out of bed. I kept repeating to myself that this would pass. Someone would come and cut us out of these mountains. Our chainsaw broke after cutting through some of the many fallen trees in our driveway, and the road around the lake to our house. All we could do was wait.

The boys invented games to play. They worked hard outside, hauling wood as their father chopped. They cared for the animals in the most loving way. They buried some every day. They told me Indian and pioneer stories of how big snows came for the entire winter, of how men survived in animal skins, of how some men crawled inside dead animals to keep warm. They seemed to be living their school lessons and cherishing every moment of this ice storm isolation and its big challenge. Their spirits soared as mine sank deeper and deeper into a state of severe depression. They watched me. I became more irrational. They worked harder and tried harder to be helpful. They did not understand my state of mind, as theirs was so filled with a sense of adventure. I wanted my comforts, and they wanted challenges.

The sixth day passed and then the seventh. No one came. There was no news. Nothing was moving in the mountains except the fox. I looked in the mirror that morning. My hair was greasy and dirty, my face ashen, my eyes dead, and my mind spinning out of control. I walked slowly down the stairs to the fireplace. I pulled a chair to the fire. My clothes were soiled from wood, ash, and cooking. I sat down and stared into the fire. I felt my life slipping away. I felt isolated and out of touch. I felt abandoned. I felt exhausted and so sad and lonely. All of my routines were disrupted. The unknown confronted me daily pressing in upon me to where I could hardly move through a room. I could not get up. I broke down into sobs and lost control of who I was. I gave myself up to the selfishness of being inconvenienced and uncomfortable. I forgot in that moment that I was their mother, and they were my children. I was their caretaker. I was responsible for their safety and welfare. I gave up, and I forgot.

They came around the corner with fresh wood in their arms. Their little faces were dirty; their clothes were filthy from the wood and the funerals. They had been hauling water from the frozen lake that morning, and they were wet. They saw me crying, tears running down my soiled face. They put the wood down and stood next to me. I told them how I could not take another day. They just stood there, they were quiet, and they listened with all their hearts and all their love. They sensed my approaching collapse, and they did not want to make a false move. I put my face in my hands, I sobbed, and my body shook. I lost control of my vision and gave in to my isolation and discomfort. They stood next to me.

I began to fall into an abyss when I felt someone touching my shoulder. I looked up, and there was Dmitri looking down at me. He said, "Don't worry Mom; we'll take care of you."

Dakus put his arm around me and said, "Yeah, Mom, we're gonna take care of you. You just sit there today, and we'll do all the work for you."

They caught me before I fell. I looked at these two young boys, one six and the other four. They were going to take care of me. They were going to do all of the work. I cried harder, pulled them close to me, and thanked them for their love and for helping me through this terrible ice storm and the loneliness and isolation it brought with it. I thanked them for their spirit and their imagination. Their comforting remarks reminded me that I was their mother, and they were my sons. They lived their lives, as most children do, with enduring strength and an ability to overcome impossible circumstances with joy and imagination. They were the pioneers.

The next day, we heard chainsaws in the distance. We waited by the kitchen window, and soon we saw Alf, the mountain man, and the rest of the crew coming slowly up the road surrounding the lake clearing and hauling one tree at a time. After nine hours, they reached us. They cleared a path for our truck.

The boys ran out to greet Alf. They told him how they hauled wood and how they cut a patch in the lake ice, so they could haul water for me. They told him about the fox and the funerals. I made "cowboy" coffee for everyone. Alf said, "Sandra, ya never looked prettier." We all laughed. Those men will never know how good they looked to me and how beautiful their chainsaws sounded. We had power restored three days later, and that was the best hot bath I have ever taken. Life gradually returned to normal.

Several weeks later, I was putting the boys to bed. We talked of the fox who ate our peacocks, the chickens who froze in the hen house with no light bulb on to keep them warm, and Sally, our cat, who slept wrapped up against the belly of Mon Ami, our black German shepherd. I turned and looked back into their room just before I left, and I remember thinking of William Wordsworth's line, "The Child is father of the Man..."

They saved me from myself in their unconditional and enduring love. They caught me before I fell.

THE BEE HUNT

8. THE BEE HUNT

Alf came to the house early that morning, about 5:00 AM.

Alf was a true Tennessee Mountain Man. He had never left Sevier County in his entire 55 years. He had no formal education. His speech was difficult to understand, for it was true Mountain dialect. I understood him, for he had worked for us for more than ten years on various projects. The boys understood him, for he had been their pal since they were born. He was a carpenter and a stone mason of profound skill. They had hammered with him, they had pulled nails from boards with him, and they had followed him as often as they could up the driveway to work on the nearby projects.

He took hold of them as soon as they could walk to 'tech 'em the ways of neture'. He would say to me, "God put us here ta t'ke kare a neture. These here boys gotta know the ways and God wants me to tech 'em." It was impossible to argue with Alf once he made up his mind.

When clouds fall down below the mountain peaks and settle into the valleys, old timers call this "ground fog". So on this early "foggy" morning, Alf came to take the boys "Bee Huntin". Dmitri was seven and Dakus was five and one half-years-old. I had packed a substantial lunch and dressed them with too many clothes. I was afraid they would catch cold.

I remember their excitement that morning. Their eyes were so alive, and they were so animated, acting so manly and grown up. I saw the pure love for them in Alf's eyes, and I saw his joy in doing "God's will". The boys would get a healthy dose of Alf's relationship with God that day. Alf flashed his toothless grin and told me they would be back before dark. The boys were headed for the woods, chasing bees, and as they looked back they said, "Don't worry Mom; we'll be back before dark." The three of them merrily walked down the driveway and into the ground fog.

"Chasing Bees", I thought what is this all about, this bee thing?

We were raising bees then. Alf insisted. The boys robbed the beehives with Alf for the first time that year. He put bee masks on them: gloves, coveralls, and boots, and then, he had them "smoke the bees". As Alf explained, the smoke settled the bees down. I stood outside the hive area, listened to their squeals of delight, and watched as the bees surrounded them. They were unafraid, because they believed Alf protected them. They played with the bees. Alf robbed the hives. What a sight these three made. I could only shake my head and thank God for Alf.

This bee hunting day was a long one for me. I worked in the kitchen and waited for the light to fade. As the sun dropped low in the mountains, I could hear heavy feet coming down the driveway. I opened the door, and there they all stood. They were a complete mess: dirty, torn, scratched, and with half the forest hanging from them. They were weary as they sang a mountain song that Alf had taught them. Their food was gone, their water cans were empty, and they smelled bad. They could hardly wait to tell me their stories of the Bee Hunt.

They described how they entered the mountains at dawn. The light was thin as Alf baited the bees. They told me how they sat quietly and waited for a bee to land upon the bait. Alf would point, and they would follow this little bee with their eyes and their feet. They had begun their first tracking experience. When they lost sight, Alf would bait again. They would sit and wait patiently for the bee to come by. Then, off they would go tracking the bee with their eyes and their feet. As they sat and patiently waited, Alf told them about God and his forest, about his animals and about their salvation. I know they listened, because I know they loved Alf.

Their hands flew everywhere as they described how they crossed streams, scaled steep slopes, climbed over fallen trees, and slogged through briars and branches. They were trackers, they gleefully told me. They went into virgin forests seeking the bees and their Queen. I could see the great myth of the Bee Hunt encircling them. Their imagination and vocabulary increased as they excitedly detailed their childhood bravery in stalking the great honeybee. I could see their little faces light up the tiredness in their eyes as they began the end of their story.

"You see, Mom, it was alive; the hive was alive in this dead tree! The bees were everywhere, and we had to fight them off; we had no gear, and they kept coming at us. Ask Alf!"

Alf had a big grin on his face. He loved these boys. He didn't say a word. He let them do all of the talking; he just watched and listened. They grabbed his big hands and said, "Alf, tell Mom. Tell her about the bees and us. Tell her about the black snake and how he is our friend. Tell her Alf!" Alf didn't even look at me. He touched their heads turned around and quietly walked to the front door and out into the night.

They looked so happy to me and so tired. We went up to their room, and they dropped their clothes on the floor. I drew a hot tub full of bubbles. They climbed into the steam together, two very tired little boys who had a big adventure. We talked as they soaked; their voices grew smaller as they relaxed in the hot water. They rinsed off and put on their pajamas. We said a quiet prayer about the bees and the black snake. They pulled their duvets up close to their faces and said, "We love Alf, Mom." I said, "I love Alf, too."

I turned out the light in their room, and as I walked down the stairs I thanked God for Alf and his love of our sons and his eternal mountain wisdom. I sat on the porch that night. I remember that the moon was full and its light shimmered on the lake. I drank a glass of wine. I had some music on, and I thought about how really wonderful it was to raise our sons in the mountains where their challenges came from nature and not their peers; where they could sleep peacefully and dream of stalking honeybees.

Their innocence would last longer here. Their childhood would last longer here. They would have these mighty challenges to reflect upon when as men they doubted where their feet had taken them. They would remember their fearlessness of the deep forest, the honeybee and the black snake. Their strength would come from their memories, for that is the knowledge we draw upon in times of uncertainty.

What they would face as men would never measure up to what they learned as children.

THE GROUSE HUNT

9. THE GROUSE HUNT

I love tradition. There is something so terribly comfortable in living within it. It feels good and warm; it feels secure. It is predictable in a time when life is so unpredictable. It offers something that we call "passing on to our children". It defines the seasons of the year and the seasons of our lives. Tradition helps us jump from one hurdle to another in life's obstacle course. It is the glue that keeps us together by making us come together. I love tradition.

Thanksgiving is my favorite holiday of the year. It was a holiday my mother always had at home. She did the cooking, and the smell of food from her small kitchen permeated the house. Those memories remain with me to this day.

It was very cold in Tennessee this particular Thanksgiving. The tradition for every Thanksgiving, since the boys could walk, was to go on a grouse hunt with their father early Thanksgiving morning. They would suit up in insulated coveralls over top of blue jeans and sweatshirts. They wore insulated boots with insulated socks, insulated gloves, hats, scarves, and anything else I could put on them. I was always worried they would "catch cold". They would ask me what that meant, "to go catch a cold?" I could never give them an explanation that made any sense, so in frustration I would say, "It's a Mom thing". Really, what does it mean to a child when we say, "You're going to catch a cold"? They would eat a hot breakfast, climb into the old red Chevy Blazer with their father, and drive off into the ground fog.

On this particular Thanksgiving Day, our sons were six and eight years-old. We performed all of our usual rituals that had gone on before with one exception. This Thanksgiving, they had to bring back the dinner. They had to kill the Mighty Fast Grouse or we would have no dinner. They laughed and felt full of themselves and looking back at me as they walked out of the door, they hurled their bold challenge, "We'll kill 'em if you know how to cook 'em!"

I thought, "My, my aren't they Short, Big, Bad Hunters." I waved merrily as they all drove down the driveway into the Mighty Big Woods. I laughed to myself as I looked at the truck. They had been waiting for this year. This was the year they got to use their guns. There they were fully decked out with bullet belts criss crossing their chests, hunting knives strapped to their ankles, and their shotguns and bows carefully stowed, just in case. They looked like the remnants of Che Guevara's army. They even were ready for the unlikely Big Bad Black Bear.

I marveled at their male instincts. I wondered if that was taught or born into them. Their bravado, their tipped heads, their challenges back and forth to each other was all so untypical of their every day behavior. They reminded me of the male peacocks who danced on our front lawn for dominance during early spring pre-mating rituals. These glorious birds would run up at each other hissing and displaying their fanned feathers, then back away and strut, feathers ruffling for the other to see. These two short warriors reminded me of these birds and I mused at how men changed when they put bullets on their chests and guns over their shoulders. They swaggered about and bantered in loud tones. They suddenly became taller, and I could hear their feathers ruffle. It was amusing.

It had to be the bullets and the guns that made them feel bigger than they were. All of that was fine, because their father had taught them from early childhood how to handle guns, clean them, load them, unload them, lock them, store them, and care for them with great respect. All of the mountain men had guns and all of their son's hunted wild game at early ages. It was a tradition. No man was careless. That was an unspoken rule. This was a wonderful place to raise two young men. They would always be safe in these woods.

I made the pies that early morning. I set the festive table. I inspected the stuffed turkey that was secretly wrapped and left hidden in the oven, just in case. I showered, dressed, and did small things. I waited for the Mighty Fast Grouse Hunters to come home with their grouse bags full. I read once where the mountain grouse was the fastest bird off the ground in the world. I worried that I should prepare the turkey, just in case.

The fires were burning in the house and the rooms smelled so good. It was Thanksgiving and food was everywhere. I heard the old Blazer truck rumbling slowly down the long driveway. Their windows were steamed and their small faces were images in the fog. I could see two mighty small heads with woolen caps. They pulled up and stopped. No one jumped out. I went to the front door and saw their legs dangling from the seat as they slid down onto the ground. They were covered in burrs and dirt and miscellaneous leaves. They looked wonderful to me. I could not contain myself as I ran out yelling, "Are we eating or are we starving?"

They puffed up indignantly and pulled two Mighty Fast Grouse out of their pouches. They laughed and jumped about shouting that I could not cook the birds. They hurled insults at me, and tears came from my laughter and happiness that they were successful. I thought it was a good thing that I had cooked the turkey their father had prepared that early morning, because two Mighty Fast Grouse was just enough for two or three mouthfuls. They cut the tails off with their father's help as Alf had shown them. They mounted the tails on blocks of wood and these became their first big game trophies.

These two Mighty Big Hunters went to the bathroom like every other dirty child in America and cleaned up for our amazing dinner. I had to read my wild game book to learn how to cook the Mighty Fast Grouse. It was not an easy task, but I never told them; they never saw the cookbook. It was a wonderful Thanksgiving dinner with many tales of adventure, which included the sighting of many small wood animals and other stray imaginings.

After dinner, they retrieved their trophies from outside. They chatted with each other about the good shots they made and what good marksmen they were. They had grown a notch and were walking straight towards the long journey into manhood.

I sat by the fire with a brandy and watched the flames dance as I imagined how wonderful childhood must be in the woods. Keeping them here in the midst of space and freedom was a difficult decision but a good one. For where in America could these young boys walk out of their front door and into the woods and hunt the Mighty Fast Grouse?

I wished for them what I never had for myself, a childhood of immense love and freedom, a childhood of exploration and defined boundaries, a childhood of passion and responsibility, a childhood filled with imagination and day dreams. They taught me so much about what I had missed that they released me from the memory of wanting what I never had.

THE FORT

10. THE FORT

One winter there was a very large oak tree that had fallen to the ground during a heavy snowstorm. The roots were turned up vertically, and they were as tall as the jolly green giant. They were twisted, gnarled, interesting, and mysterious. They were the kind of roots that lent themselves to gentle imagination and contemplative thought.

Dmitri and I were walking through the woods in the early spring when we came upon this sculpture. We stopped and looked at its immensity. How amazing it was to see the bottom of the mighty oak when all we had ever seen was the top. It was as if we were invading the gentle secrets of this modest tree. It looked so naked and helpless. It wasn't dead yet, but we could tell that it would not survive. We were so small compared to this mighty oak. There was nothing we could do to help this immense situation. We stood there for some time and then continued on with our walk into the woods. We both fell as silent as the tree.

There was something so profoundly sad about that mighty tree lying on the ground that the intent of our walk together changed, and we became introspective. The woods were so quiet that we could almost hear our thoughts. As we walked, we were trying to find a way to think life back into the tree. Several weeks passed, and I began to notice things missing from the garage and art room. First, the car cover, which was rarely used, then scraps of carpet, and pieces of fabric. Some of the storage boxes were opened, and various items were gone: pots, utensils, dishes, and candles. It was curious. I became distracted by the many activities of life in the household and forgot to pay attention to the details of the garage. Time passed.

Weekends that fall were glorious and colorful, and there was great activity in our small school as four new students joined our little group. We were happy to have them for their diversity and energy. They all were gifted in some way. The holidays approached as the leaves began to drop. As the foliage became bare, the views opened.

While walking up the driveway, one fall afternoon I could see the roots of the mighty oak at the edge of the forest. They were hidden all summer, and now they were visible and partially covered by a blue cloak. I walked up the steep hill and back into the forest of trees, which engulfed the roots. I reached the fallen tree. I was amazed at what I saw when I arrived.

The root sculpture was surrounded by the most delicately laid plan of protection that I had ever seen. My blue car cover cloaked the roots, old blankets covered the ground, odd pieces of various and assorted paraphernalia lay ordered about the forest floor under the covered roots. I was struck by the obvious care that went into the plan of this loving fort. It was a dream fort that every boy had in his childhood.

I had tears in my eyes and a smile in my heart as I walked away. The sun was dropping fast, and the evening became cold in its absence. I shivered as I walked back to the house. It was good to enter the warm kitchen. Dmitri looked up from the homework table and asked, "Where were you, Mom?"

"I took a walk to the edge of the forest and visited the fallen oak." He stared at me. He didn't say a word or blink an eye. He waited calmly for the next move from me. They knew not to remove things from the garage. I sensed that this moment in time would make a difference about the construction of all future forts.

"I saw the loveliest fort surrounding the edge of the old oak tree. Did you know that it was there?"

"I built it", he said. "The tree was dying, and I did not want it to be alone. It was a good place to have for my friends and me. It was our secret hideout. What do you think, Mom?"

"I think it is comforting not to have to die alone. You have done a good thing."

He returned to his homework, and I turned to my kitchen. He brought our discussion up years later, and we laughed about the crazy quilt of life that surrounded the tree. The Forts he built later were constructed from within. They were strong and sturdy. They withstood the trials of growing pains, peer pressure, and identity.

I thought about that night many times as he grew older. I remembered thinking how it is a good thing not to have to die alone.

THE SCHOOL

11. THE SCHOOL

Energetic, curious, creative children involved in the journey of continual discovery do not understand the concept of waiting until they are seven before they may enter their first grade at school, so they can "learn". Why do we tell them at their most curious moments, "Wait until you're older"? If adults do not like "waiting", what could the word "wait" mean to a two or three-year-old child? I wondered in those early childhood days how small ones comprehended "wait" when their minds were charging forward at full speed.

I believe that children meet our expectations, so mine were high. I knew that our sons were too young to know their limits, so we pretended they were limitless. When their childhood dilemmas had them looking at me with perplexed expressions, I nudged them towards a direction of discovery through my questions. They eagerly responded and journeyed to where the questions led them, leaving their dilemmas in forgotten places.

We couldn't "wait", so we opened a school, which we happily called, "The Children's School", whose motto was, "If we can think it, we can do it". Our school began in the two car garage, which was attached to the office. It was redesigned for intellectual and creative development. We made one side of the garage a library and reading room. We built shelving to store books and teaching aids with a table and chairs in the middle of the U shaped space. We had a drop down screen for our projection needs and 3 bays for our Apple computers, which were the rage then. The other side of the garage was for music, physical education, and the sciences. We used the kitchen for our cooking, nutrition, and health instruction. It also became the place where they dissected their biology projects. Then, we took the last space in an outside garage and turned it into an art studio where all imaginable bits and pieces of worthy trash filled our homemade shelves. These treasures were destined to be turned into magnificent works of art that hang to this day in our homes.

The Children's School was a place for young minds to explore their curiosity and to form their questions. Many of life's problems are the result of an inability to ask the right questions. We focused on questions. I continued in those days to be amazed at their unquenchable curiosity and vivid imagination. Each had his individual approach to life, and each had to be educated with those idiosyncrasies in mind.

There were mornings I sat at the kitchen window and watched Dakus, our youngest, walk down the gravel driveway to our school in the garage. It was about a short city block walk, and I could see him all the way. I sat there with my coffee steaming while I gazed out the window at his very unique experience of "going to Mom's school". He began very determined to get there on time. His little legs carried him as far as the first distraction, where he slowed down and then came to a halt. I observed his distractions every day. Some mornings it was a butterfly, some mornings it was a creepy crawly or some odd thing in the gravel, and some mornings his daydreams took hold of him, and he stared into the universe.

He began in earnest and with all good intentions of arriving on time to school. Quite spontaneously, the temptation to leave the path and his enormous curiosity and love for the freedom of the beginning of his life overcame him. I admired his determination to do as I asked while at the same time battling his strong impulses to do what pleased him. I watched as his impulses won. He found his questions along the way and brought them to school with him. When he arrived at our school, he asked the teacher with his charming little smile, "Am I too late?" He was never too late. All of his life, he has been on time in his journey.

Our eldest son was there when he was supposed to be. He was eager to begin his plunge into the academic mysteries of life. His curiosity was insatiable. There were no distractions as he walked down the driveway toward his goals and his destiny. He was clear in his path and certain in his purpose. He loved butterflies, too, but they were clearly discernible as a part of his natural world. His walk to school was focused and determined. He was unstoppable. He would satisfy his questions by discovering the answers through his intellectual pursuits.

His silent intuitive nature would lead him to where he was supposed to go, and he would find what he was supposed to find. All of that would happen when it was supposed to happen, and he was content in his childhood wisdom. He was a little old man trapped inside a child's body. I knew that he would struggle to climb out of this body. I also knew that his path would be long and sometimes lonely. Profound men and women spend much time within themselves as they meet few individuals who comprehend their nature.

I knew them well, because they came from me. One distracted by the mysteries of life and the other trapped within himself with perceptions beyond his years. I knew their paths had to be carefully cultivated. Their curious, dynamic minds had to be saturated with knowledge and the experience of learning. Their personalities were powerful. I had to be mindful of their energy and their love of life. I had to provide them with the challenges life had to offer, or they would turn in other directions to satisfy their inquisitiveness and their energy.

We stayed busy at The Children's School in order to meet their demands. We began at 8:00 am and concluded at 4:00 pm. We had one hour for lunch and two fifteen minute breaks. Our art lessons were scheduled every Sunday from 12:00 pm until 5:00 pm. I hired practicing artists to teach a different art medium each semester. Our art studio shelves were filled with gallons of colorful paint we bought at discount stores, huge foam core boards, clay, plaster, fabric, paper, crayons, pastels, dyes, buttons, thread, cardboard, unused tiles and bits and pieces from everywhere imaginable. Saturday was for gardening, fishing, sail boating around our small lake, hikes in the woods, or other mystical adventures. Every day of the week was filled with energy and exploration.

Our curriculum, which was ever changing as the school developed, started with the basics of reading, writing, which included poetry and essays, and arithmetic skills, which later included basic algebraic concepts and geometry. As their questions grew, we added biology, chemistry, computer skills, history, geography, music, nutrition, gardening, health, small wood animals and domesticated fowl, physics, and astronomy to name a few subjects. If they had a question, we developed a study course that explored their question and answered it.

I will always remember the day the worms came through the mail in a plastic bag. Nancy York, our miracle teacher, decided that it was time to begin dissection. I watched as they gleefully dug their hands into the soil and pulled the worms out of the bag. They could hardly wait to go inside these primitive creatures and discover the miracle of their existence. They were three and one half and five years old then. They were studying concepts that I studied when I was fourteen and in Mrs. Young's 10th grade biology class.

There was no hesitation as they attacked each day with great enthusiasm. The worms got dissected, then the frogs, then the cow hearts that they brought back from their trip with Nancy to the local slaughter house, "Got this heart for free Mom!" they told me. They treated these experiments as thrilling, interesting explorations into the unknown parts of life that were accessible through their limitless curiosity and their teacher's flexibility and dedication to educate. There was never a time that I didn't leave the Children's School and thank God for the inspiration that he provided me to keep it going. When financial times were rough, and I couldn't see how we would continue, somehow the funding appeared and Nancy and I pushed forward, again.

We built a chicken coop up on the hill above the school. Alf, the mountain man, supervised the construction. We bought chickens and The Children's School started a business called "Cluck, Inc." Nancy had them set up their accounting records on their Apple Computers. They advertised in our little mountain community and began selling eggs by the dozen to our neighbors. Each morning, they would collect the eggs from the coop after feeding the chickens and box them in the cartons that the neighbors gave them. After school, they set out on their delivery route. They were businessmen, just like their Dad. They began to understand in a rudimentary way the basics of caretaking their chickens, the product, advertising, marketing, the logistics of warehousing and delivery, the costs to produce and deliver, and the calculating of their profit and loss. They got to keep their profit when there was one, and that was a big motivator. We got so excited about the chickens that soon we were raising turkeys, guinea hens, peacocks, ducks, and geese. As we experienced chicken attrition from time to time via the fox, who lurked nearby in our forest, reproduction became essential to sustaining product, volume, and sales.

Spring and its mating season rituals on our front lawn were a real eye opener as they walked to school in the early morning. I remember Dakus stopping dead in his tracks once. As I watched from the kitchen window, he climbed up onto the lawn, which was elevated above the driveway by a foot, and sat quietly as the peacocks danced and performed their mating ritual. When their dance was finished, he got up, jumped back into the driveway, and proceeded on to school.

I brought up the dance at dinner that evening. I tried to discuss it delicately, and in the middle of my explanation, he said to me, "Mom, there are just some things you can't talk about, because it ruins it." He was five at the time. I will always remember his observation and how much he taught me with that statement.

Their interaction with the animals on our property and in our school instilled in them a gentleness and compassion that were touching to observe. Animals are dependent when they are in our domestic care. They depend upon punctual feeding, consistent grooming, and a healthy environment. Animals need love and consistent attention just as children do.

I watched as the relationships our sons had with our many animals became personal and caring from birth to death. They had a small graveyard on the hill above the school where little stone markers were laid to commemorate a fallen friend. Sometimes there were short services spontaneously held to express the heartfelt losses for these small friends and to release their childhood sadness and grief. I saw in these small animal events the neophyte beginnings of an understanding of the transitory nature of life and its opposite, death. They carried the experiences of these profound small lessons and losses into their manhood where this kind spirit drew people to them. Gentleness, compassion, caring, and kindness are childhood lessons.

We had a plot of land that I tilled for my garden. It was adjacent to the garage that became The Children's School. When they were toddlers, we planted everything that would grow: corn, potatoes, tomatoes, cucumber, scallions, eggplant, squash, lettuce, spinach, peppers, watermelons, cantaloupes, onions, and garlic to name a few. The boys loved watching buried seeds sprout out of the ground. There were times when their impatience would drive them into the garden to see if anything had come up yet. They were fascinated with the concept of a little seed producing a huge living, edible thing. When they were very small, we would pick our vegetables, clean them, and jar them in the kitchen. Food looks delicious in glass jars.

We decided to turn the garden over to The Children's School when they expressed an interest in watching plants grow. They were older, but they had never forgotten their early experience with gardening. We developed a lesson plan that included a study in the nutritional values of foods, vitamins, minerals, and their impact upon the growth of the body. We further expanded this into the study of food preparation. They would bring their fresh garden produce to the kitchen and prepare their lunches. They developed a fondness for cooking that is present in their lives to this day. They used the honey from the beehives as a sweetener and drank the various fruit and vegetable concoctions they made in the blender. This early education in food nutrition and preparation, as basic as it was then, created a lifelong appreciation for good eating and good health. They had no cavities, saw no doctors, took no antibiotics, and had sound bodies and healthy minds. They were alert, mischievous little boys.

The night skies are so clear in the mountains, dark and luminous at the same time. It was here in these dark nights with no city lights that our sons developed a fascination for the heavens and the immensity of the universe. I did not have the answers to their questions. When they could not stop looking up at the skies, we began our study course in Greek Mythology and the constellations.

This was a fascinating time, for I became as interested as they in their course of study. Somewhere in my early childhood, I missed out on mythology and constellations. This natural study for children has the power of myth, legends, and gods all wrapped into the night sky. They were soon pointing out to me Taurus, Leo, Andromeda, Cassiopeia, Centaurus, and Hercules. We loved to say "Cassiopeia" together. We would sit at night, look up at the sky, and talk with excitement about the legends that ordered the skies. It was they who taught me. I was fascinated with their knowledge, understanding, and enthusiasm. These nighttime adventures became the basis for the beginnings of their personal understandings of the great forces that operate within the universe. It was here, while looking up into the heavens, they began to develop the beginnings of their personal spiritual journeys.

They became curious about dinosaurs, as all children do. We created a field trip and took them to Dinosaur Valley in Utah. They were struck, as I had never seen them. Their imaginations equaled the size of the creatures they admired. When we returned to Tennessee, it was time for a new semester art project. They decided that they each wanted to build a Tyrannosaurus Rex.

We hired Victoria, an ex marine and a sculptress. She was large, loving, affectionate, and exacting in her art. It was she who developed a sculpture program that small boys could implement. First, they conceptualized their vision into a drawing. From this drawing, they created a list of materials that it would take to build their T-Rex. Victoria took them to the local lumberyard to buy the building materials, and then, to a fabric store to purchase the burlap. They ordered the plaster, and their father ordered the steel for the frame. On one amazing Sunday afternoon, all of the materials were assembled and ready for their sculpting experience. They helped build the plywood base that would hold the sculpture. They measured, calculated, and Alf cut the wood with an electric saw. Everyone hammered and nailed the pieces together. It was now time for the steel frame.

Jimmy, the welder, took their drawings and welded the steel rods into a sturdy frame that would hold the chicken wire, burlap, and plaster. The steel rose in the air, and the structures were tall and formidable. They were so small against the frames that I wondered if this project had grown too big for these young boys. Then, they reminded me that, "If we can think it, we can do it."

Alf built the scaffolding for each T-Rex. Dmitri's T-Rex was sixteen feet high from the top of the head to the feet and Dakus' was twelve feet high. They climbed the ladder to their scaffolding platform one day and began their dinosaur journey. They shaped the chicken wire to the steel frame, they cut the burlap, they soaked it in their plaster mix, and they applied the fabric to the wire. Each Sunday when their lesson ended, all three of them were covered in plaster, and I mean from head to toe.

They worked tirelessly for twenty-four Sundays, six months, on this project. And then, suddenly, one Sunday they finished by gluing into the mouths of their creatures the fierce wooden teeth they had cut out. We all stood there in awe looking at these gleaming white dinosaurs. Who would have thought that these two small boys could construct such a mighty sculpture from their imagination?

Alf put the sculptures on skids, and WC drove the bulldozer, which dragged them up the driveway and into the lawn above the lake, where they remained for more than ten years. We would look out of the kitchen window and see their gleaming white skins against the foliage and the green lawn. Imagine two T-Rex dinosaurs in view every day from your kitchen window. What a spectacle! What an accomplishment for two children, who were then six and seven and one half-years-old.

After the dinosaurs were in place, WC took his bulldozer home, Alf left, Nancy kissed the boys good bye, Jimmy shook his head in disbelief, saying that no one would believe this at Hatcher's Diner, and Victoria sighed. She said that she would never have an experience like that again and was so grateful for having had it with "D & D". She climbed into her truck and slowly drove off around the lake waving wildly at the boys.

Our family walked around the lake to the house and back into the kitchen. We all looked through the window at their gleaming white dinosaurs standing tall in the lawn. They were covered with plaster, and they were very tired. A big huge project was completed that day, and I sensed their feeling of loss mixed with some sadness and great pride.

As I tucked them into bed that night, Dmitri said, "I will miss Victoria. I will miss the dinosaur. I feel sad that it is done. What will we do tomorrow, Mom?"

"We will have to conquer Mt. Everest."

"What is Mt. Everest, Mom?", Dakus asked.

"The tallest mountain in the world."

"Mom, would it be okay if we did that next week? We're so really tired."

I fell into their beds, all of us squealing, tickling, and trying not to be the first one to shout "Uncle".

They confirmed that night that all things that can be imagined are possible. I have carried the lessons they taught me throughout all of the years we grew up together and into this latter part of my life, where I continue to imagine the impossible.

A year and a half later, when Dakus was seven and one half years and Dmitri was nine, they went across the mountain to public school. They were advanced by two grades and took their background of knowledge with them into the extraordinary vegetable soup of life.

If we could think it, we could do it, and they did it.

BALANCE

12. BALANCE

Balance means centered. A see-saw, like life, must have its weight distributed evenly at either end to achieve balance. Balance between the emotional and the mental and between the physical and the spiritual allows small feet to enter the center of the circle of life.

I thought about my own life as a child. It was a life without center, without balance. It was a disciplined life out of necessity, but it lacked balance. It was a life of emotional tumult. That is a difficult life to live, bouncing from one end to the other never hitting the center, never knowing balance.

I did not want this for our sons. I wanted a centered life for them, one that encouraged thoughtful and compassionate decisions. Most of my years were squandered in search of balance. I did not want their time wasted. The emerging competitive world they would live in required a bull's eye. They had to hit the center of the target when they aimed and pulled the bow back.

Karate.

This was a sport that required mental discipline, emotional balance, physical agility, and spiritual enlightenment. It required individual diligence and focus. Karate required the delicate integration of the whole human being. They could enter that sport raw and emerge with balance.

I heard of a man named Phil Little, a tenth degree black belt and International Grand Master in the martial arts. He was a respected master in his discipline of Isshinryu Karate. He had studied under Harold Long, an ex marine who had brought Isshinryu to the United States from Okinawa, where he had trained with its founder. We arranged a meeting with Phil. We were impressed and invited him to join the Children's School once a week for a three-hour session to teach Isshinryu Karate. We began the process of balance with this disciplined man.

Phil was devoted to his sport and a dedicated teacher. He was patient, compassionate, and prepared. He looked at these two small boys and began a three-year private Isshinryu school with them. They were his only students up in those Tennessee Mountains. It was serene there, a place of quiet contemplation.

We integrated one hour of practice each day into the curriculum, and then we had our three-hour session with Phil each week. The first day, they put on their white Gi's, I stepped back in awe. As young as they were, I could see their demeanor changing as they stepped barefoot out onto the floor. Phil towered over them as they began their warm up exercises. His presence at 6'4" commanded their immediate attention. They began their first day of warm ups, looking into the face of balance. They had a long journey ahead of them, and they had the time to take it. Youth is for learning.

They began with white belts, the lowest. Isn't that where we always begin each endeavor, at the lowest point? Our home school teacher, Nancy, decided to take Karate lessons with them. She bought a Gi and worked out every day with the boys. She felt they had to have her companionship as they did their warm ups and Kata practices. Our physical education program became a serious part of our curriculum on a daily basis, and it required their full focus. This physical education would be life-altering in its subtle influences upon the balance of young minds. Their three-hour session with Phil each week required progress into each level of achievement in this demanding sport. He expected their best, and they tried earnestly to meet his expectations.

They worked hard. They dressed every day in their white Gi's and approached the floor with serious faces. They entered a moment of meditation and then began their warm up. When the Kata began, its grace, form, and balance told me they were where they should be.

They brought determination and energy to their class and practices. Because they were so young and impressionable, they acquired Phil's sense of intensity toward this discipline. They were awkward when they first began their Katas, unsure of their footing and balance. Their minds would wander with uncertainty. Gradually, their physical balance caught up with their mental sense of coordination. Over time, I could see the merging of their senses. They began as gawky, uncoordinated boys. Within one short year, they were connecting their minds to their bodies, growing taller, and becoming physically confident.

Phil began each lesson with the history of the martial arts, the Isshinryu philosophy, terms, definitions, and oriental philosophy. He used the blackboard to draw his Kata diagrams and warm up instructions, always making sure his students knew the logic for his plan into balance. After this instruction, they began their warm ups.

The day came when Phil thought they were ready for their first Isshinryu tournament, which was held at a local high school gym in Knoxville. I knew nothing about karate outside of our Children's School. I was unsure about competitions at such an early age. I did not want winning to replace the delicate philosophy of balance and confidence. They were excited about the prospect of testing themselves with children from other schools. They insisted they could not know how good they were until they were measured with others. I relented, and off we went to our first competition.

Their father packed the old Chevy Blazer with all of their gear and paraphernalia. I packed "nutritious food". Everyone groaned. Off we drove to Knoxville to find the school gym where their first competitive challenge was to occur. We all thought that this was going to be a local, small town competition with only a few children.

We were shocked when we entered the gym. There were several hundred children of varying ages. They were sitting in small circles all over the gym floor. They were grouped according to age. Phil came over and guided them to the gym floor to warm up with some of his other students, who were all in their teens. After warm ups ended, Dakus went into the group of six and under. Dmitri was in the group of nine and under. The judging instructors, all very formidable, took their places in front of each group, and the competition began, all over the gym. Harold Long supervised as the competition progressed.

Each child in each group performed specific skills and Katas. They were rated based upon their performance. We sat in the bleachers and watched in amazement at all of the children who had taken to this sport. Their demeanor was intense and respectful.

There was no frivolity that day. All we could hear were the sounds of karate kicks as each child had his turn to demonstrate his achievements in the sport. The little ones were so special and so serious. An entire gym floor filled in white. What a spectacle!

The judges turned in their competition sheets and as the scores were tallied we waited breathlessly. Soon after, the judges conferred and the awards ceremony began. As hard as I tried not to care, I could not overcome my anxiety. I wanted them to win so badly that I was embarrassed by my feelings. I was the one who thought competition was unhealthy at such a young age. Here I was about to fall apart, waiting for the announcement for their groups.

Dakus took first prize in his age group. We were overwhelmed when his name was announced. I screamed and cheered, hugged his father, and cried. Dakus stood and approached the judge. He was so little in his white Gi and adorable as he shyly reached out to take hold of his trophy. The trophy seemed taller than he as he held it tightly and returned to his seat on the floor. He looked up at us and flashed a great big, huge smile as he waited for his brother's group to be announced. He was so proud of himself, in his mind a "winner".

Dmitri's group was announced, and he took no prize. When he was passed over, I could see his anguish and disappointment. He wanted to win, and he did not. I had never seen him so crestfallen. My heart went out to him, and I cried deep inside for his disappointment. I wanted him to win, too, as my competitive spirit took control of me, the one who initially resisted this competition. He looked bewildered. I felt his pain and his feeling of rejection, and my heart sank as I knew this feeling from my own childhood. We took him aside and discussed the lessons of winning and losing, the philosophies disappointed children do not understand but are planted there for later years. Nothing we could say consoled him. Loss is interpreted as rejection. This is difficult for adults to reason, how does a child make sense of this powerful feeling?

It is difficult to have one who wins and one who 'loses'. A big trophy on one side and a cloud of dejection on the other, joy and sadness all wrapped into one Chevy Blazer. My heart broke just to look at his small, sad face. I knew then that this was just the beginning of a life of competitions within groups and sometimes with oneself. This is what I dreaded about competitions, the feeling of not measuring up to standards established by others, the feeling of being less.

The best competition is the one within, because no one loses there. Progress is measured over a lifetime, not in a single moment. Although those single moments of triumph feel so good and so exhilarating, they are fleeting. Internal personal progress may not be noted with a burst of loud applause, but it is the most enduring and the most fulfilling.

On the way home, we discussed all of this with some seriousness and some laughter. We applauded Dakus for his moment of triumph, and we sympathized with Dmitri in his disappointment. We concluded that he had to focus on his form and balance. I am not sure that made a lot of sense to him at the time. We were parents, and it was our best effort to comfort him while at the same time feeling a deep sadness for him. We tried to quietly illuminate a path to winning the next competition. We knew there would be another competition.

Halfway home, we threw out the "nutritious food" and stopped for a Big Mac and French fries. This nice distraction helped. We all fell into our own worlds for the remainder of the trip into the mountains, me with my thoughts of winning and losing, Dakus with his thoughts of triumph, and Dmitri with his thoughts of resolve.

Class resumed the next week. In those years that followed, Phil took them on to many competitions. Dmitri collected five first place trophies; Dakus collected six. They prevailed.

The Children's School closed its doors one December day, and Karate ended. Phil went on to other challenges. That January, the boys joined the vegetable soup of life by entering a public school across the mountain. They took their balance with them. They needed it there.

THE MEDAL

---

13. THE MEDAL

He was eight and a half-years-old, and the age was nine to get into Space Camp in Huntsville, Alabama. I believed that mental age, not chronological age, should allow entry into life's early educational adventures. In this amazing technological century, I felt it was important for our children to be about the business of saturating their intellectual curiosity. To hold them back based upon age was to deny them scholarly access into the most important and formidable years of their lives. They were growing up in a highly competitive and crowded world. They needed to begin their investigations and experiences when their maturity demonstrated a readiness for the journey.

Our oldest son requested a Space Camp brochure, and when it arrived, we all looked at it with anticipation. It excited all of us. Dmitri wanted to attend. Dakus wanted to, also, but his six and one half years was stretching it a bit. I filled out the application and fudged a bit on the age part. We mailed it, and Dmitri was accepted several weeks later. We celebrated, went shopping, and began to pack the necessities.

We were jubilant as we piled into our Chevy Blazer that Sunday in July. Space Camp, what an adventure! We had about a seven-hour drive ahead of us. I packed lots of food and games. We were a merry bunch, so the drive did not seem long.

We arrived at orientation with about seven hundred other parents and their children, who were between the ages of nine and eleven. Rooms were assigned, and we unpacked. We put the sheets, blanket, and pillow on the bed. We sorted clothes out in his assigned locker, and then, we began meeting some of the other students sharing the dorm. The counselors were older, in their late teens and early twenties, and appeared to be competent. The dorm was a beehive of activity. Dmitri seemed comfortable with his first time away from home.

We shared our hugs and kisses and left Space Camp about four in the afternoon for the long drive home. My heart was heavy as we drove away. It was difficult to leave him behind in the hands of strangers, but my intuition told me this separation from the mountains was important; this was the right moment. He needed this experience and this challenge. His active mind and keen intellect were growing restless. I saw him in the rear view mirror as we drove away that afternoon. He looked so small standing there waving good bye. Tears came to my eyes, and I remember thinking how it was always my instincts that drove these decisions. What if I was wrong? I prayed all the way home, hoping that these maternal instincts were accurate, as they often caused me great anxiety.

I soothed my anxiety by recalling that there was not much in our small Tennessee community that offered him the stimulation that he needed at this age. One of the disadvantages of living in the mountains was that we had to seek outside challenges in order to keep the minds and spirits of our sons engaged.

We arrived home at eleven that evening, tired from the fourteen-hour round trip and eager to get into bed. The phone rang. It was Dmitri, and he sounded terrified. He begged us to come and pick him up. He had never been in the company of so many different people from all walks of life, religions, and ethnicity, and with so much noise. We lived a quiet and somewhat isolated mountain life. I melted, and my tears flowed. Before I could weaken, his father grabbed the phone and said, "Pull yourself together, son. We have driven fourteen hours. We are exhausted. You will not come home. You will stay there, and you will participate in all of the activities. You wanted this. We will see you on Saturday. "

A stern look was thrown my way as the phone was handed back to me. I asked Dmitri to let me speak to the counselor. I explained the "first time away from home thing". The counselor understood and said she would have Dmitri call the next night. I waited all day for the night to come, so I could hear the phone ring. The counselor called, and it seemed that Dmitri had withdrawn that day. We talked to him again, and I said, "You must finish what you have begun there. You wanted to go, so now you must stay until the end. We will not be back until graduation on Saturday." He sounded very sad. I filled with guilt and doubt. I did not sleep well that night.

He did not call the third night, and we were unable to call him, as they had no phone number for the pay phone outside his dorm room. We were out of touch. The silence was deadening. I did not sleep that night.

The week dragged on slowly. Each day passed, and there was no word. I grew more anxious as no calls came. He reached out, and we had denied him. I became distraught and dark inside. I felt torn and helpless. I could not sleep.

Finally, Friday came, and we three left late for the drive to Huntsville. We decided to stay at the Marriott that night and arrive at Space Camp for the Saturday morning ceremonies fresh and rested. We were anxious to see our oldest son. My guilt and anxiety forced a rushed breakfast on all of us, which wasn't very pleasant. Upon finishing, we immediately rushed off to Space Camp.

We entered his dorm, and there he stood dressed in his Space Camp suit along with all of his other dorm mates. He looked taller. He was busy organizing a group and did not have time to see us. The students and their counselors had a full morning schedule, and much to my disappointment, we barely spoke as all of the last minute rituals of Space Camp had to be attended to. The awards ceremony was scheduled for early afternoon.

We were surprised that we could not be with our son and that his day was planned up until the last moment. We toured the center with other parents and waited for the time to take him home. My anguish had taken control of me that long week. All I could think of was my need to talk to him.

Everyone, parents, student campers, counselors, Space Camp administrators, and various dignitaries gathered in the auditorium for the Space Camp awards. We just wanted to get our hands on our son and go home. We wanted to talk to him about his experience. I wanted to apologize for having made such a bad decision of sending him away so "young". I was distraught over my terrible miscalculation. I looked across the auditorium and saw Dmitri smiling and talking to his friends and the counselors. He seemed so different than the young boy who had called six nights earlier.

I reluctantly settled down and the speeches began; first one award, then another, and then more speeches. I was so restless and anxious that I did not hear a word. Finally, the most important part of the ceremony, "The Right Stuff" award, was about to be given to the worthy recipient. This is the most prestigious honor given at Space Camp we were told. It is voted on by all of the counselors and given to the camper who exhibits "The Right Stuff" while in the Space Camp experience. It was carefully explained by the speaker that this award honors that individual who sets an example for others to follow, who perseveres through all obstacles to achievement, and who exhibits a caring attitude towards his fellow campers.

I was growing restless and wanting selfishly to rid myself of my guilt and doubt. I was very tired from the long week of no communication. My self-absorption was interrupted by the Space Camp dignitary who said, "...and so we would like to honor the recipient of this year's 1986 Right Stuff Award, Dmitri Gunn."

There was loud applause, whistling, and cheering. Everyone stood. I was shocked and could hardly believe what I heard. We three were stunned as we turned around and watched him walk down through the auditorium in his blue space suit to receive "The Medal". He smiled with pride, he looked taller, and he was honored. Was this real? Could he have done this in the quiet of his calm reserve? I wept, as only mothers do.

He was the youngest, and he did the impossible. He conquered his fears alone. He drew from the strength that resided deep within his nature, and he persevered. He earned the respect of his peers and his leaders. He had "The Right Stuff"!

The ride home was joyous. We chatted, laughed, and teased. All of the anxiety of the preceding week melted as snow when the sun comes out. I felt energized. My guilt receded as I applauded my instincts. I did make the right decision. I was relieved as my many doubts ebbed out of my weary mind. I slept deeply that night.

In this last third of my life, I look back at his courage and his ability to march into the future with perseverance. I marvel at how he picked himself up from fear and turned it into victory. I think of Dmitri's courage and strength and marvel at how children make rainbows.

THE STARS

14. THE STARS

The nights are dark, really dark in the mountains. We have no streetlights, no city lights, no lights from anywhere. We look up at the stars in the mountains and see their lights from the dimmest to the brightest. We see all of the stars in the night sky, every night.

We three used to lie on our backs on the lawn on an old quilt looking up at the sky on clear summer nights. We could smell the flowers in our gardens. Hyacinths were our favorites in the early spring. Our sons knew all of the constellations, and I knew none of them. We lay there, and they pointed them out to me. They explained the myths surrounding the stars, and I listened, enraptured. They knew so much, and I knew so little. Our school had taken them beyond me, and at times, I became their student. We talked of our dreams and what we wanted to be when we grew up. We talked of life and love, goals and our determination, all of this while looking at the stars.

When they grew out of my home school and went to public school across the mountain, we talked about physics, matter and energy, and the universe on our long drive home after school. Their father drove them to school in the morning. I am not a morning person. He awakened them with a soft whistling sound that I am sure will ring in their memories for all of their lives. They dressed in the clothes that I laid out for them the night before. He made their breakfast, usually fresh oranges and grapefruit sectioned by hand, fresh eggs from the hen house, and bacon from the pig he bought and had slaughtered every spring. They sure did love his bacon! I canned fresh apple sauce each summer from our orchard, and he would mash their vitamins with a mortar and pestle and mix it into the sauce. I was at the door to kiss them good bye and to watch as they drove down the driveway to cross the mountains to attend public school.

I picked them up in the afternoon. The drive across the mountain was narrow and treacherous in places. It took an hour to cross over into the next county where they went to school. We each drove two hours a day to get them to where they had to be. We divided the drive, and that made it bearable for each of us in our busy professional schedules. I don't know how they felt about it. They did not complain.

I remember when they entered public school, they were tested and each skipped two grades. Dakus was seven-years-old and in the fourth grade. I was seven-years-old when I skipped two grades after we moved from the north to the south. I knew well his inexperience and insecurity among students larger and older than he. His stature was small when measured against his classmates. Dakus had a challenging road ahead of him.

Dmitri was tall and blended in. In spite of their challenges to fit into this new life, they loved being with so many other children. I remember the principal telling me that if they were to come to public school, this was the best time as they were not yet in middle school where strong cliques and allegiances formed. They could adapt here in elementary school, blend into the forming groups, and become a part of their school environment. Even with her good advice, it was very different for them. Their classes were distinctly separated by subject matter and not interwoven. They moved to various classes when the bell rang. They could not ask spontaneous questions. They were part of a larger setting and had to wait their turn, and if time ran out, they did not get a turn. They were teased by some for their talents and intellect and scorned by others for their differences. I had forgotten that space for the talented and gifted in public education is small.

Each Friday after school, we drove to Knoxville for their music lessons. Dmitri played the piano and Dakus the violin. Their teachers were Russian Jews who had escaped Russia with their lives and Lev's violin. On the way to Israel, they changed lanes and went to New York. The Knoxville Symphony needed a violinist. Lev Belenky auditioned and got the job. Galina came with her beloved Lev and she taught private piano lessons to ordinary students who she made into extraordinary pianists. Galina taught Dmitri, and Lev taught Dakus.

They were intense, devoted teachers. They were demanding masters of their art. They kissed, hugged, and touched the boys at every lesson. They cajoled and shouted and got the best from each of them. The boys began with scales, and in seven years, they were winning competitions in England.

I remember the time when Lev was dying of cancer in the hospital and lying motionless in his bed. We came for a piano lesson to their small apartment and Galina insisted after Dmitri's lesson that we go see Lev. Dakus brought his instrument and music to the room at Galina's urging. Lev sat up in bed so happy to see this little one. His face changed, and he became the violin teacher again assuming his huge stature as a professional musician with his small protégé. He opened Dakus' music and began his last lesson with Dakus in that hospital room. Dakus played so beautifully for Lev that afternoon. His notes filled this dimly lit room with music, and the sweet sound of his violin ignited Lev's broad smile. His passionate Russian eyes radiated his love for Dakus.

The nurse came in quietly and asked if we would leave the door open so the other terminal patients on this floor could hear Dakus play. Tears filled my eyes as we watched this little boy playing at the instruction of his dying teacher. Lev's spirit filled the room that night. His passion for music flowed through his student's violin. Two weeks later, Lev died and left a hole in all of our lives.

Dakus loved Lev beyond my understanding then. He began violin when he was five, and Lev was his mentor and friend. Dakus did not understand that he would not be seeing Lev again. I explained that death was a movement from one life form to another, like a caterpillar becoming a butterfly. I explained that Lev would never be dead as long as Dakus picked up his bow. Where there is memory, there is life.

His sorrow was more profound than I knew then. He had no teacher as he continued to practice his violin each evening with me. He went to piano lessons with us every Friday. Galina would try to help him with his violin, but she was not Lev. He practiced one year without instruction before we found another local teacher. There was no one with the warmth and passion of Lev. He continued to practice every day, trying to teach himself from the music collection that Lev left for him. Galina recommended another Russian violinist who had been Lev's friend in Russia. He lived in Baltimore. Out of desperation, we went to Baltimore once a month for lessons with Lev's wonderful friend who played for the Baltimore Symphony. The traveling outweighed the results. Dakus finally asked one day if he could begin piano lessons. He began lessons with Galina but continued to practice his violin each night along with his piano. He would not let go of the memory.

Time passed, and we kept our music schedules. A letter came one day, and Dakus was asked to audition for a violin scholarship in a British school. A friend of the family heard him play and recommended that the school audition him. I packed up the family and off we went on an adventure that changed Dakus' life. He met and auditioned for an extraordinary man named Alan Broadbent. He, too, was a man of passion. He listened to Dakus and witnessed Lev's achievement. Dakus played with soulful feeling and a love of the instrument. He got the scholarship and left for England when he completed the eighth grade. He was twelve, once again the youngest student in his class.

During the five years he attended school in England, Dakus found time to compete with musicians of all ages, sometimes winning and sometimes losing but always pushing his talents forward. He began his own rock band when we bought him an electric violin at his request. His band entertained the school at various concerts. Since he was the inspiration, the band dissolved when he graduated. He took trips with school musicians each summer. They rented houseboats and played in churches up and down the Broads. Sometimes they would leave the boat and play in the streets with open cases. They collected money for their simple pleasures. We chaperoned twice, and one summer, they even included me by allowing me to play my tambourine in several of their church concerts. Dakus kept his eyes on me and would nod his head when it was time for me to bang my tambourine against my hand. Sometimes he would grimace when I missed the beat. We laughed so much when the trip was over and in years to follow at my complete inability to keep the beat. I told him I was so nervous being a guest soloist with this very impressive orchestra.

Learning to play the violin was hard work, very hard work. It took many hours of practice over twelve years of study. It took great determination and discipline. It was frustrating in the beginning and at times extremely tiring. There were many Friday nights when he fell asleep in the back seat of the car as soon as we began the long drive back up into the mountains. There was the discouragement of competitions that he lost and the exhilaration of competitions he won. When he won, he was renewed and we would carry on. There were times when he had to make decisions between his music and what his peers were doing that seemed like more fun. He made the hard choices and chose music. No one knows, except another musician, the demands and sacrifices that are made at such an early age in order to masterfully play a musical instrument. Dakus knew the hard choices, and I will always remember him making those decisions and trusting in my counsel. He will always be able to open his case on a sidewalk anywhere in the world and play for change. He will never be poor as long as his life is filled with music.

When we lay in the lawn looking up at the stars, he was too little to imagine the possibilities, but as he grew up those influences from his early childhood began to coalesce into goals. He won the greatest competition of all by becoming his dreams. Lev's music will live in him forever, and his children will carry that music with them into their generation and on into the next. It is the responsibility of each generation to improve the next.

Where there is memory, there is life.

Where there are stars, there is light.

THE RIVALS

15. THE RIVALS

I thought they would love each other from the moment they saw the other. I thought they would be eager to play and have a friend in the other. I thought they would be companions, buddies, chums, mates, pals. My concepts of "Brotherly Love" were illusions. It was a job that I had not expected. The molding of the brotherly bond took full time vigilance and careful thought.

Their father's brother had betrayed him, and my father's brother had betrayed him. Both stories are too sad to tell. I was determined that these brothers would break this sin-filled cycle. I prayed this curse would not move into the next generation.

I saw Dmitri's sad and sometimes angry expressions in his early baby pictures. His brother would be smiling while he would be frowning. I did not pay too much attention to these early signs of jealousy and inconvenience. I thought that because they were brothers from the same mother they would love each other. To my great surprise, this love had to be taught, learned, and sometimes threatened into them.

They began life together in the same bedroom. I thought that if they had to live together, they would draw close to each other. As in nature, the bigger the size, the more dominant the animal. Living in the same room did not help the situation; it just crowded their space for growth.

The fights were endless.

"Mom, he touched my trucks!"

"Mom, he hit me!"

"He hit me first!"

This cacophony pierced each day, day after day, year after year, from the time they could walk.

We built another room with a half bath. I thought they should at least have to share the same shower. I thought it was necessary for them to bump into each other at the end of the day.

Things seemed to settle down after each had their own room. Then, the fights began to spill out into the hallways. One day, I saw Dmitri push Dakus down. I rushed into the room and pushed Dmitri down and said angrily, "How does that feel?"

He was crying in his disbelief that I would push him so roughly. He said, "You hurt me; it hurts!"

His little five-year-old tears broke my heart, but I remained firm. "Good! I am glad it hurts, because that is how it feels to your brother when you push him down!" I looked at both of them, "Every time I see one of you hurt the other, I will hurt you in the same way. There will be no fighting in this household unless I am the one who picks the fight!" They nodded in quiet surprise. "You are brothers, and you will love each other, or I will die trying to make that happen. Is that understood?" They both nodded with a different kind of awareness of my determination. The lines were drawn.

As they grew older, the physical fights subsided. The verbal fights began. They discovered that words could be more piercing and hurtful then jabs. Physical pain healed, emotional pain lasted longer. As I watched and listened, I had to change my tactics; I could not push them anymore. We had moved into a subtler arena, one of words and intellect where age created an advantage for the oldest child.

I could feel the hurt in Dakus when his older brother told him to go away. I could feel his pain at every rejection, and I could see that his older brother was unaware of this pain. The youngest always bears this pain. They are looking for acceptance, not rejection, so they do not often fight back. They walk away silently and find something else to do. Sometimes Dakus would find that something else to do with me, and when he did, I spoke of brotherly love and how it would come.

He would reveal his troubles to me, and I would tell him to wait, that love was worth waiting for. I explained to him that the oldest does not see that the youngest looks up to him with admiration. I explained that the oldest always has it the hardest, because he is the first. He is alone in his first encounters. The oldest is the one who walks into the unknowns of childhood with no experience and no examples. The oldest is the one who goes in front of the youngest. The youngest benefits from the experiences of the oldest. The oldest paves the way for the youngest, whose life is not alone because he has the oldest to observe. He listened.

I felt so involved in the conflicts that I took them aside one cold, rainy afternoon. There was nothing to do, so we built a fire. I told them two sad stories of betrayal, two brothers betrayed. They listened. I am not sure they understood all of the nuances of the story, but I felt sure it would sink in over time. It is important to plant life's seeds early, so they have time to germinate. I told them that history should not repeat itself with them.

They did not grasp the concept that afternoon. Years went by, and I observed only the smallest movement. I spent endless time reinforcing my lessons in them. I never knew if the lessons took root. Love like this takes time to grow when it begins as a seed.

They grew into young manhood, and Dakus was barely a step behind Dmitri in every way. Dmitri went to an English boarding school first, and then, Dakus followed one year later. I'll never forget Dakus at our hotel dinner the night we left Dmitri in England. He looked at his meal. With tears rolling down his face he said, "I will miss my brother, Mom. It will be lonely." He was right; it was the loneliest year of Dakus' life.

Dmitri's year was filled with disagreements and jousting, British class prejudice, lonely struggles far away from home, isolation, no friends, no one to talk to. We bought him a fax machine, and I wrote every day. He kept his problems mostly to himself and carried on with grace and dignity. They missed each other's company, and I saw that. I am not sure they saw it.

Dakus went to England the next year. He was the youngest in his class, and Dmitri knew the ropes. Dmitri paved the way and gave him some clues to boarding school survival. It was not an easy place to be when you are a minority. They learned a lot about prejudice and hate those years. They grew to loathe prejudice and reject hate. Neither of these primal emotions was ever a part of their upbringing. Their isolated mountain upbringing fostered self-reliance, resolve, and character. Individuals of weak character embrace prejudice and build walls of hate.

Dmitri, the American, began a basketball team and organized an inner school league in the midlands. He found uniform sponsors and was voted captain of the team. He became captain of the shooting team. They competed in the British National Rifle Association meets where they pitched their tents in open fields and slept in the wind and cold and where the rain turned their turf into muddy shooting competitions in the morning. This American won second place individually for four years against hundreds of young British boys. In his final year, he missed first place by one hundredth of a point. He became Head of House, which is an honor bestowed upon a young man in his last A Level year by the Housemaster of the residence house. He won four piano competitions and numerous scholastic awards. He set the pace for his younger brother.

He built the bridge upon which his brother could cross over. I know that the youngest felt at times that he was not loved and that perhaps he felt rejection when none was intended by the oldest. The youngest does not see that the oldest often is struggling to hold his head above the water line. He is on his own with no one to build bridges for him. The youngest is looking for overt support and a show of love while the oldest is immersed in self discovery, the resolution of inner conflicts, doubt, and his own insecurities. In those days, they lived worlds apart, and of different minds and needs, sharing the same blood. I watched and knew that some day they would turn in the same direction and see each other for the first time. I only hoped that it would be before I passed. My prayers and my one sustaining dream was to have them feel the exhilaration of walking through life back to back covering each other and feeling the embrace of triumph and the taste of victory as a team.

Dakus joined the track team and became their most outstanding javelin thrower. He became Head of House, won three violin competitions and one piano competition. He organized a rock band and played for school events. He was the recipient of the highest math and science awards. He made three A's in the British A-Level exams. He toured the continent as first violinist in an orchestra and played solo pieces. He and his school team won a media award and were asked to show their presentation to King Ferdinand of Greece when he toured the school. He met the challenge and created his own path. There was no one to follow him. He was the youngest.

I prayed the cycle was diverted and that they were marching towards each other in brotherly love. There would be the occasional setbacks that would negatively impact their perception of each other. Their youth and inexperience misinterpreted the unintentional deeds of the other. The youngest often felt the most pain from these clashes. The oldest lived in a world which the youngest would never know. The oldest would never feel the pain of the youngest. There was no way I could explain these complexities to them. It did not make sense to them, so I watched and waited as I knew they were as different as the sun and the moon.

Dmitri was accepted to MIT and Dakus followed. They joined the same fraternity but walked down different paths. They had occasional experiences where their love for each other would fold in upon itself and bring them together for a moment. It then would subside under their busy lives. There were times when Dakus' expectations of his brother were unmet, and he was disappointed, sometimes bitterly disappointed. He was unaware that his brother traveled his own life and had no expectations of him. Because he was the oldest, his view of Dakus was only what he saw each time they met. He did not depend upon him for strength or acceptance. He loved him as he was, because he did not know him any other way and what he saw was completely acceptable to him. He was the oldest, and his view was simple. He was not disappointed with unmet expectations – only bewildered when Dakus grew distant. There was no way to change or reasonably explain these different perceptions that were brought to my attention years later. It seemed that the time had passed for me to add clarity to this brotherly situation of the youngest and the oldest.

They lived in Boston for five years. One day Dakus decided to move to the west coast. He packed his few precious possessions, and Dmitri went to say goodbye. I called Dmitri that evening. He was quiet. I asked how he felt, and he told me, "Saying goodbye to Dakus was hard. I cried after he left. I will miss him Mom." I am sure that first year without Dakus was one of the loneliest years of Dmitri's life. They had been together for more than twenty years when they separated in Boston. Now, they are on their own, finding their path without each other and growing in different directions. I am waiting.

I told them long ago they needed each other. They each had qualities that the other lacked. They were like a hand in a glove, each balancing the other. One was as calm as the sea. The other as torrential as a storm. The sea needed storms and the storms needed calming. Individually, they would accomplish great things. Together they would share great happiness and some sorrow. They would be a mutual support that shores the weakness of the other. They would always have the strength of brotherly love to take them through the tribulations and joys of life. I know these things. All mothers know these things.

Love is a wondrous thing to behold.

Love is worth waiting for.

THE ART SHOW

16. THE ART SHOW

Space, volume, dimension, color, texture, form, pattern.

Seeing, feeling, tasting, hearing, imagining, thinking, expressing, creating.

Joy, enthusiasm, fearlessness, experimenting, doing, acting, reacting.

Our first year of art school began with Lillian, a young French art student who studied in New York City at the Cooper Union. I placed an ad in the New York Times newspaper and she responded. It read, "In need of an art student to teach the beginnings of art appreciation to two young children in the mountains of Tennessee, room and board for the summer and a small stipend, all expenses paid." She called, we spoke for a while and she was hired. I liked her voice, her accent and her warmth. She flew into Tennessee and arrived at our home in a flurry of excitement. Dmitri was almost five and Dakus was three and some. After Lillian settled in we sat and talked about art and its potential for adding subtle and lasting dimensions into the lives of children when experienced at an early age.

I believe life has rhythm, color and form. Inner rhythm changes and matures as the human grows within the music of his spirit. Each spirit has color and form. Color intensifies and form takes shape as children are encouraged to experiment within their boundless self-expression. When we eliminate rhythm, color, and form from our schools, we have children whose music is barely audible, whose color is grey, and whose form is shapeless. When we deny children the creative outlet for their self-expression, they become imitators rather than originators. They become spectators rather than participators. Originators and participators have depth. Depth is developed through the trial and error of self expression. It is not enough to know the multiplication tables or to write a legible sentence. Intellect is unbalanced when it is unaccompanied by creative expression. The spirit is as important as the mind if our children are to be balanced and compassionate.

Lillian and I spoke most of the night. We agreed upon this basic philosophy for the development of the creative spirit within our fledgling art school. We made a list of the supplies needed to begin our adventure. She began by stocking our supplies in the garage shelves that Alf made, rough and sturdy, just like him. We made two long benches and took a large picnic table and cut off the legs, so small people could sit comfortably. Since Lillian welded and constructed huge sculptures at Cooper Union, she did all of the construction preparation to get our "Art Studio" ready for her pupils. We all participated, and the fun was endless those days, everyone with hammer and nails and lots of enthusiasm.

It was a fantastic summer, filled with laughter, rhythm, color, form, and lots of music playing from our cheap cassette tape deck. Lillian began with a huge roll of white butcher block paper she put on a wooden rod, so she could tear off the sizes she needed. The three "amigos", Lillian, Dmitri and Dakus, went to the local hardware store and convinced them to donate their gallon buckets of unwanted acrylic paints, the ones that are mixed and rejected. Some really awful colors were unloaded into our art school shelves that day. They met a painter in the hardware store, and he donated his old brushes. How could anyone turn down these three amigos, a beautiful French woman, a pint sized boy, and a toddler? They were quite the trio as they went to various stores within our small country town, asking for remnants to be donated to their art school. They came back with bits and pieces of fabric, old tile, various rolls of thread, buttons, yarn, cardboard, plaster, wire, magazines, glitter, old paint sets from the Good Will, and many other odd and eccentric items. They filled their shelves to get ready for their amazing summer with Lillian.

I relied upon my instincts and intuition, which guided me into this enterprise. I worried about making the right decisions for them, which were based solely on my faith and love of art. I had no experience in early childhood development. In light of my insecurities regarding this decision, I was unprepared and joyfully surprised with their enthusiasm and lively sense of adventure. I had no idea how this journey into self expression would alter their perceptions, and I am sure they had no idea how all of this "stuff" was about to transform their lives. It was exciting for them, and it looked good on the shelves, but they had no idea what it all meant. Children are so trusting and accepting.

Lillian insisted that Dmitri draw on large 3' x 4' sheets of paper. She felt that children should have huge painting experiences, with big brushes and big buckets of paint. "They should know no boundaries", she said in her lovely French accent. Dmitri was short, and the paper was tall. It was laid the length of the picnic table. He would run from one end to the other with his brushes splashing bright colors everywhere. He had color on him, on the floor, on the paper, on the walls, on his brother, on the shelves, and on Lillian. His glee was unimaginable, similar to mine when I was his age and rushed to greet the Good Humor Man. I strongly related to his excitement and anticipation.

His first paintings were colorfully simple and childlike. As he grew accustomed to size and technique, he began to change his perspective and the composition on his big pages. They became theme-like in their organization. Suddenly, images would appear. He called one painting 'airplane', one 'giraffe' and another 'man'. There they were just as he imagined and painted them.

Dakus was a toddler, and his first projects were created to introduce him to art from the sensory point of view. He sloshed through the colorful buckets painting himself in beautiful hues of rainbow colors. I have a photograph of his dipping his hand into a bucket of red paint for the first time. He had on a big blue cap, and his face and its expression is a treasure as he looked awestruck and mystified, totally enthralled that his hand changed colors. There is nothing in this world more honest than a child experiencing something for the first time. I wish each day could be a first time for all of us. Imagine that!

Lillian's art plan moved from butcher paper to large 4' x 8' foam core boards. She braced them against primitive easels and took these new enormous canvases out of the garage and into the gravel driveway under the sun. She set out all of the buckets of paint with paint rollers. Rollers flying through paint buckets onto their large foam core canvas, laughter, paint fights, music, and Lillian stopping their painting when they were about to make a leap into a possible destruction of beauty, and then lunch. There were no scheduled naps or break times. If they were tired, they would just lie down on the carpet in the garage studio and rest until they were ready to begin again. There were lots of snacks, juice, and hugs. Lillian was a very affectionate and loving young woman with her two students. They returned her love by creating art, which delighted her. They painted their way into the most amazing expression of self that could be imagined. We still have their paintings to this day. We stored them and carried them with us into every adventure and move we made in our lives. We cannot live without them, and they surrounded us in homes we moved to over the years.

Lillian bought reams of discounted colored tissue paper from the Dollar Store. They tore this paper into strips of all different sizes. They arranged and pasted the colorful strips of tissue onto long pieces of butcher block paper and created sun bursts of color collages on these 3' x 6' white backgrounds. Lillian cut wooden dowels and they attached the top of their tapestries to the dowels and hung them from the ceiling. They floated in the breeze and gave the most ethereal appearance when the wind blew through them. We called them fairy wings.

Plaster sculptures came next. They were made with wire and steel, which Lillian welded together to make forms. They did two very large 5' x 8' abstract pieces, which were placed in the lawn in front of the house, and two smaller ones which were placed in the house along with the plaster casts of their little hands and feet. Everyone needs to dip their hands and feet into plaster when they are children. This makes great gifts for mothers. Those casts sit in our hall entrance. They are heavy, and I have tried to throw them away more times than I can recall. Here they are still facing me in the morning. What is it about the gifts that children give you that make them priceless?

Paper mache mobiles hanging in the entry, small clay objects strewn across our home, wall plaques of pieces of scrap wood from construction sites with patterns of nail heads hammered into them, small masks of plaster and paint, lovely small pastels, and patterns of string on make shift looms all became mementos of the most memorable and creative event in our family history. There never would be a time as memorable as that summer. Its energy, creativity and harmony would be paralleled but not duplicated.

The time was nearing for Lillian to return to the Cooper Union. We all sat in the art room one evening and tried to think of a way to commemorate our great journey. She suggested we have a one and a half man art show on the property, half because Dakus did small half art. I was thrilled with the idea. We were building a small office structure on the property at the time. It was unfinished on the inside but complete on the outside. We decided this would be the perfect place to hang all of the art created by two small boys that summer. Who would we invite? The boys set about to make a list with Lillian, and I set about doing a construction cleaning on the inside of our "gallery".

Lillian and the boys made their invitations from sheets of colorful construction paper folded in half. Dmitri did a large last painting and then tore it in many pieces. He and Lillian pasted two pieces each on the front of the invitation with his name signed by her at the bottom of each design, "Dmitri '80". She wrote on the inside flap, "This is a little piece of my painting. Come to my house – look all I did – mommy said August 23rd from 3:00 to 6:00 – children can bring their parents – ice cream, drinks and snacks, Bye, Bye, Dmitri" The boys mailed them to our friends on the list they made. More than 30 people came that day.

I had taken slides of the many art school activities and their art work as they progressed. These slides were developed into a multimedia projector presentation with a dissolve unit and music. As the images dissolved one into the other from the two projectors, music would be playing in the background. We set the automated projection show up in one of the unfinished offices. This was a huge success as the guests could see where the boys began and ended each project.

Lillian and Dmitri decided they needed to bake a cake for the occasion. I have never seen anything like it in my life! They made cup cakes, sheet cakes, round cakes, square cakes, thin cakes, fat cakes, croissants filled with chocolate, and Lillian's famous cream puffs. They took all of the cakes and shapes and put them together into the most amazing castle-like structure held together with different colored icings, green, raspberry, chocolate, vanilla and yellow. They then put candy corns on top of the towers and little cookies made in the shape of a train around the bottom crossing over the rocky cream puff foundation of the castle. When they finished, they were covered in batter and icing. Dakus got to lick the bowls with Dmitri. They had the castle cake on a large cutting board, which they had to drive to the "gallery". It was a center piece that every guest marveled at when they entered the room.

While they were baking, we were framing the many pieces of art. We worked long into the night after little boys go to bed. Then three days before our big show, we all began to hang the art. When we finished, we all stood back and looked for the first time. We were touched and moved to tears at the art of our children and this intimate peek into their small spirits. I sat down in the unfinished bay window as tears streamed down my face, and I hugged them lovingly for their perseverance and joy, for their commitment to an idea, and their willing participation to the end. I cried for Lillian's unbelievable artistic talents and creative projects. I cried for myself and all the things I imagined as a child that went undone. I was overwhelmed by that summer that never stopped until that moment when I sat down and looked at the results of our sons' creativity and imagination.

Children have wings; we need to encourage them to fly. They will go to unimaginable places.

THE GARDEN

17. THE GARDEN

When I was a small child, we left all that I knew in my somewhat insecure world and moved to a place that was unfamiliar and hostile in my child's mind. I had only the security of my troubled family. I remember in those days feeling very lonely and isolated. I had no safe harbors in which to drop my anchor.

It was difficult being uprooted and relocated. Children become accustomed to their familiar surroundings, no matter the condition. They like seeing their toys in the same place each day. It comforts them. It is dependable. It is this sense of object identity that secures them within the space of their family. My objects were dislocated, I had no sense of belonging, and I felt lost. I began to pull weeds in the yard of our new house. Something out there in the dirt comforted me. It helped me to cope with the absence of my former life and its important objects that were no longer a part of this life.

My father rewarded me with a Popsicle each evening after dinner. I saved the Popsicle sticks. They were precious objects to me. My mother used to save string. One day, I took my Popsicle sticks and her string to a patch of dirt that I had cleared in the side of the yard. My father told me that if I planted beans, I could grow bean stalks. He gave me some beans. I think he was trying to help me replace my loneliness with a living project. He was a gardener once in his life, before he became a warrior.

I dug five neat rows of holes and placed my beans into the holes. When I finished covering the beans with the dirt from my garden, I built my fence with my Popsicle sticks and string. My father told me to water my garden each evening when the sun went down, so my beans would drink in the cool of the moon. I woke up each morning and went to the garden, eagerly looking for my stalks. Children have little sense of time, so I expected the stalks to grow the next day. I remember on some days sitting at the garden thinking those beans would grow by my watching and wishing.

One day I met two friends, Rita and John. They lived down the street. They rode their bicycles up to me and told me we could be friends. I wanted to be accepted and eagerly showed them my garden. In my mind, I thought that if they saw my garden they would think I was special and worth knowing. Rita was fat, and John was short. They looked at my garden and laughed at me. They said, "You can't grow beans in this yard, stupid!" They hopped on their bicycles and rode away. My father saw my pain and told me to wait; the beans would come up just as he said.

I was finally rewarded one morning. There they were – little, bitty, round, green things peeking up from the dirt. It was a day of great celebration. I am able to recall to this day my happiness. It was the most exciting, wonderful thing I had done in that unfamiliar place. I couldn't wait for the stalks to get bigger than me.

Each day they got taller, and pretty soon my father helped me to tie them on long sticks he made. I didn't know about fertilizer, so they were a little scrawny, just like me. Rita and John came by each day to look at my garden with me. They would say things that hurt my feelings and their taunting became miserable for me. However, the joy each night of watering and the joy each morning of watching my beans grow taller overcame the misery of their bullying. One day they came by, and I proudly pointed to my first beans on the stalks. I was enormously proud and feeling very accomplished. They were silent. I remember it well.

I woke up the next morning, filled with anticipation. I was going to pick some of the few beans and have them at my dinner that night. I came around the corner and found my garden destroyed. My fence was broken and thrown to the side. My stalks were pulled up and mashed. Everything in my small plot was gone. I was shattered, as shattered as a small child can become. I cried. I was inconsolable in my loss. My garden had become my one achievement in that alien world.

Rita and John came by that day and laughed when I showed them my garden. I knew they did it. They rode off, and I cried some more. Fat Rita and Short John showed me the way of the world that day and left a lasting impression. Future gardens would be cultivated and harvested in safe places. I remember escaping some of the pain by falling into the joyful memories of my garden and how exciting it was for me to see something I planted come to life.

I never outgrew that beanstalk memory, and when my sons came along, I told them how exciting it was to watch something come to life from a small seed. We decided to grow a garden. They were so little, just like I was, when we planted our first garden together. Their father cleared our first garden and tilled it with rich dirt. We went to the local hardware store and bought toddler size hoes, shovels, and rakes. We bought our seed and fertilizer. We bought tomato, cucumber, squash, lettuce, onion, watermelon, and cantaloupe plants from the farmer's Co-op. We bought beans, too. We would be growing bean stalks, again. I wanted them to feel the same exhilaration of creating life just like I did when I was their age, but this time would be different. This would be joyful, and we would eat our harvest together. Gardening is hard work, but it is rewarding work. It is something anyone can do anywhere that Fat Rita and Short John are not present.

I love digging in the dirt. Gardening is therapeutic and relaxing. It is a communion with something greater than us. Children naturally take to it, and I wonder why we don't offer gardening to them instead of video games and television. It is a miracle to see something take life and grow large from something so small. Children are awed by these natural things. They fill with pride and a sense of accomplishment as they watch their garden come to life from beneath the earth.

We took up our hoes, shovels, and rakes and went to the garden their father had prepared for our small project. We had our seeds and plants. We dug rows with our hoes for the seeds and holes with our shovels for the plants. We planted the seeds just about an inch below the dirt and carefully covered them up. Then we took some time to throw seeds at each other. We put the vegetable and fruit plants in the ground. We worked each morning and each evening until we finished our planting. It took time to plant and to grow, and that is something small children find difficult comprehending. They want to see it happen at once. I explained the time it took for my beans to peek out of the earth. My memory was so clear of that first garden and its joy. I wanted to pass this joy along to our sons.

We watered each evening, so the seeds and plants could drink in the cool of the moon. We walked to the garden each morning to see if anything was peeking out at us. They were so disappointed, just as I was so long ago, when nothing happened for what seemed like a very long time to them. I knew what was coming and how patience, care, and hard work would be rewarded. Then, magically, one morning there they were just like they were for me in my childhood, the beans peeking just above the surface looking up at us and us looking down at them. Their joy was immeasurable, and my memories were rewarded. We hugged each other and talked about how great we were to have this idea of a garden. They became ardent in their work. We talked of harvest time and "puttin' by" as the mountain people called it.

Our lives became filled with tending our garden that summer. We picked fresh tomatoes and cucumbers for our salads, dug up potatoes, cut lettuce, pulled scallions, and picked squash. We had fresh corn off the stalks, beans, and peas. We ate fresh cantaloupe and watermelon for breakfast and lunch. We steamed many pots of beans for our dinner. We talked about how the old timers relied on their gardens to survive in the winter and that maybe someday it would be important for them to know how to do this, so their families would be able to survive, too.

As the end of summer came and fall approached, we harvested our crops and jarred as much food as we could from our garden. We made tomato sauce, whole stewed tomatoes, catsup, sweet pickles, sour pickles, relish, jams, jellies and other assorted interesting concoctions. We loved seeing our food in glass jars. We put them on the kitchen counter tops so we could see our harvest every day that winter. It was so rewarding for them to pull a jar off the counter for us to cook for dinner each night. We were happily dirty all summer and smelled like food all through the fall as we harvested and jarred that first year.

They grew up eating the labors of our gardens. It was a joy they carried with them into their adulthood, just like I did. Children are intrigued and captivated by growing things. They love to watch the cycle of life as it begins, flourishes, and ends. It brings an understanding of nature and how they fit into the universality of their world. Children begin to understand the concept of caring and tending, of patience, of reward, and of harvesting. This communion with nature encourages inner peace and stimulates thought. A gardener respects life on many levels. It is difficult for them to plant a seed, watch it grow, and then destroy its life before it comes into full bloom. Gardeners live to harvest.

To this day, Dmitri's favorite scent in the early spring is the hyacinth we grew in our flower beds. We three used to pick them for our flower vases, and the scent would fill the house. That scent brings back the memories of his childhood, and he smiles. He often goes to his garden and weeds when the stress of life becomes absorbing. Once, when he was having a difficult time with an event in his life, I phoned and asked how he was doing. He said, "I am digging in the dirt".

I knew what he meant.

THE TREE HOUSE

18. THE TREE HOUSE

Their father moved his business into the house, so he could be with his sons. He did not want to miss a moment of their young lives, as these were the sons we were told we could not have. He looked at them each morning with wonder in his eyes and cherished each opportunity to participate in their emerging lives. He helped answer their cries, change their diapers, feed their hunger, ease their fevers, wash their bruises, and kiss their 'boo boos' with 'bambaids'. His big arms held them close when they needed comfort. His loving patience supplied an abundance of confidence and security in nourishing their young lives. They admired their father and loved him back with the passion that only children possess.

He was a builder. He loved moving earth. He loved construction. Since his office was in our home, the boys had free access to him whenever they needed his attention for their childhood quandaries. They would climb up on his lap and he would hold them while he worked at his drawing board. He answered their questions, discussed their dilemmas, and soothed their fears. They only stayed for a moment. Then, when they felt saturated with his love, they would hop off his lap and run towards some other passion that captured their attention.

As they grew older, their curiosity overcame them, as they played around his drawing board to see what he was doing there. He showed them plans he made for his houses. He told them how houses were built and how the process began. He explained how dirt was moved and how the foundation was developed. They were interested and came back often to watch. He bought each of them rulers, pencils, drawing paper, and a small drawing board, so they could help out. They believed they were equals as their drawing tools were the same as his. I watched and thought, 'This is how a son learns his father's business.

They had read a book on tree houses in our Children's School. They were intrigued with the pictures and the idea of a small place of their own. They came to their father and asked him if he would build them a tree house.

He said, "No, but you can build one."

Their little faces were crestfallen. Their father said 'No'. They could not conceive in their imaginations how they could build a tree house. It was such a big idea. They thought only fathers could build tree houses. In their minds' eye, this was too grand for them to accomplish. He stood firm in his refusal.

The school year was coming to a close, and Nancy, our teacher, was searching for a summer project that allowed them to use their math skills while she was away on her short vacation. When she heard that their father suggested they build their own tree house, Nancy was delighted. She immediately enlisted their father as her co-conspirator in the idea of the "Tree House Project", and they developed a plan. Alf would be their teacher and the superintendent of construction in the "Tree House Project". Their father would supervise and guide the conceptualization of the building plan, the construction costs, and specifications. The boys, to the best of their ability, would design and draw the tree house on their small boards. Their father would teach them to do a 'take off' of supplies they would need for the project. They would help write the specifications for the materials and do a cost estimate in a computer program their father would design with them. Alf would take them to the lumber yard, and they would buy the materials and haul them back in his pickup truck. Then, they would build their own tree house.

They were ecstatic! They were going to be builders just like their father. He was their hero! One evening after dinner, the three of them walked up the driveway to the edge of the woods. They selected the perfect tree around which they would design and build their tree house. It was a tall Maple tree that had three trunks with a single root system and was growing in a small ravine overlooking the house. I remember the sparkle in their father's eyes and the joy in their small faces when they all went to the office the next day to begin the conceptualization and design of their first tree house.

They worked earnestly every day. They discussed their building site, its limitations, and interesting possibilities. Their father pointed out their challenges. They sketched, drew, and redrew, thinking of new ideas, and then drew again. He patiently guided them through the experience, so they could realize a bit of success each day. They decided not to disturb the ground or the tree, so they designed their Tree House to sit up in the ravine on stilts. They wanted an octagon shaped house with windows and a front screen door. They wanted a small deck on the front and a few steps that they thought might be wood planks. The three trunks of the Maple tree came up through the center of the floor and through the middle of the roof, where the canopy of the tree shaded their house. The tree was in the middle of the house just where their imaginations thought it should be. They explained to me that this is why it was called a tree house. It made sense to me.

I wish I had those drawings now. They were priceless. For a while, they were nailed to the tree in the tree house. They got rained on, sat on, ate lunch on, and nailed on while the house was under construction. They disappeared when the house was completed. The tree house survives to this day, 23 years later.

During the design of the project, they learned the concept of drawing to scale with their rulers and how to do a floor plan. Their father studied their drawings with them, and then, he did the final plans, the roof elevations, the front, and back elevations. He patiently explained how important accurate drawings are for estimating construction costs. He did not want them to think their drawings were unacceptable. They built a computer construction model for their materials under his guidance. They listed all of their materials and quantities for their project. Their father explained to them that he needed their budget estimate before he could approve the project. This was a lot of information for two little boys to absorb. They nodded enthusiastically and looked for Alf, so he could help them do their materials cost.

Shortly after the plans were completed, school began again, and the tree house plans became their new math and design project. The plan was for them to work two hours each afternoon with Alf. This experience would replace physical education and some other outdoor activities. They would be outside working hard, measuring, carrying lumber, sawing, nailing, holding things up, putting things down, and moving things around. When this project reached completion, their math and other educational disciplines would be integrated into a new dimension for them. Their tree house would be a physical manifestation of their knowledge and skills. It would reinforce everything we held of value in our Children's School.

The action of learning is lasting and memorable when education is combined with real-life applications. Students begin to understand and respect the importance of knowledge, and their lives are transformed.

One bright sunny day, Alf drove them and their list to the lumber yard. They shopped for their materials. Dmitri read the prices, and Dakus wrote them down. Alf did not read or write, so they told me what a big help they were to Alf that day. Children do not see limitations in people they love, only possibilities. They returned with their list filled out. With their father's help they calculated in their computer program the estimated costs. He explained the costs were too high. They studied where they could achieve cost savings and slashed their budget in good practical places. They produced a final budget, which their father approved. He advised them to be at the project site on time each day and not to keep Alf waiting, as his time was valuable. They were elated beyond description. They could not wait to begin.

They went shopping with Alf and their print-out computer program to buy the beginnings of the tree house. They thought it a good idea to put the wooden posts in the ground first and then the floor boards. They explained to me how this was the support for the 'TH', as they called it. They told me in no uncertain terms that the foundation was the most important part of the "TH". I was awed by their new authoritative description of the plan.

Alf's old pickup truck was loaded to the top with all of the posts, lumber, nails, concrete bags, glue, and miscellaneous supplies they needed for their floor to begin. I watched as they jumped out of the cab and began to help Alf unload the supplies. They covered their precious cargo with a tarp. They explained to us at dinner that night that the tarp protected their supplies from blowing away or getting wet. I smiled and laughed with them, our little men. Their father nodded with quiet approval, and they felt so proud.

That next afternoon, they put on their tool belts, the ones with places for a hammer, screw drivers, nails, and other assorted construction things. Their father supplied them all of the necessary tools, so they would feel authentic. For a young child, nothing takes the place of authenticity. This makes the experience meaningful. I packed their lunch box, and up the hill to the edge of the forest, they walked to meet Alf and begin the construction of their tree house.

Alf loved these boys like his own, and they built by his rules. He controlled all of the power tools. They would work as a team under his direction. Those were the rules, simple. Occasionally, Alf would take the time to thank God for his divine guidance, so their house would be strong. They began their first day laying out the building site with string, so they would know where to dig the post holes that would support the floor and the house. They had shovels, and Alf had his posthole digger. They began their house.

Their first day was a mighty success, as we learned at dinner that night. Alf dug the holes. They made sure all of the dirt was out of them with their shovels, so they could put the posts in the ground. They explained the holes were bigger than the posts, because they had to have room for the concrete they would pour around them for strength and support. What a big mouthful of uninhibited excitement that first day!

The posts went up, and we had a celebration at the site. A level floor was their next challenge. They measured, Alf double checked, and then, they cut each board to go around the three tree trunks. They learned how to use a level, so they could nail each board in place. It was a tricky assignment, and their father came by to look at their progress. Each board had to be cut circular on one end, so it left room for the tree trunks. They had to be close to the trunks, so the floor could be sealed against the trees. Alf told them the house should be without cracks to keep out bugs, wind, or rain. It made sense to me.

Next came the tilt-up framing. They built each section of the stud walls on the ground. They laid out the first wall section, nailed the studs together, and framed the window. Alf and his helper lifted it from the ground up to the floor. They nailed that section to the floor stud, and we had a wall with a window space. That first section was a miracle to see, and we celebrated again. They had juice, we had wine, and we all cheered at their amazing success. Alf thanked God, his personal companion, for 'keepin' these two 'younguns' healthy. I loved it when Alf prayed out loud to the heavens. It had a way of helping me to keep my feet on the ground.

They worked every day with a joy that is inexplicable for math studies. Feet, yards, inches, fractions, multiplication, division, addition, subtraction, square, round, circumference, diameter, triangles, rectangles, cubes, hypotenuse, volume, and space. They learned math without realizing they were learning math. Up went the walls, then the roof, then the windows, then the siding, then the door, and then the plywood floor. Alf helped them put a rubber boot in the roof hole where the tree reached through to the sun, so the roof would not leak. When the house was complete, we put their precious tree house stuff inside. They joyfully had their private space, something we all need, that they proudly conceived and built.

They did it! They built a tree house. It took six months and lots of amazing creativity, energy, determination, and dedication. There were times when they felt tired and wanted to postpone this adventure. Their father told them, 'never begin what you cannot finish', and so they pressed on and persevered to the end. The result was one of the most rewarding and creative accomplishments of their small lives. This experience influenced them on many levels. They consciously and subconsciously absorbed the belief that they could accomplish their dreams. They subtly grasped the concept that knowledge was a powerful tool which would unlock these dreams. They applied our school philosophy of the action of learning to their lives, and to this day, there is little they cannot fix or construct in their imagination and their world.

We so often think that success is straight A's, a college or advanced degree, a title, a large salary, acceptance to someone else's world, or a material display. These external things are the external world's rewards for conforming, which often require doing what we are told to do. During our lives, we do not often stray into our dreams or our visions of possibilities. Sadly, we are not often taught the application of the action of learning, and we lose the skills of integrated survival. Our lives are scattered, and the bits and pieces of our memorized knowledge are forever floating in our heads unattached to solutions.

It is exhilarating for the human spirit to live the creative, entrepreneurial, determined life. It is important for the human spirit to understand that all problems have solutions and that knowledge is the tool that enables us to find those solutions and fulfill our dreams. It is important to connect learning to applied action. Whatever the price, it is worth it.

We look for shortcuts. There are no shortcuts. There are only compromises.

THERESA'S ORPHANS

19. THERESA'S ORPHANS

There was a man walking along the beach early one morning. Many starfish had washed up upon the sand and were stranded. He picked them up as he passed by and threw them back into the sea. A jogger came by and stopped, "Are you crazy? There are so many starfish stranded in these sands; you'll never make a difference."

The man looked up at him as he threw another starfish back into the sea; "I made a difference to that one."

This is the story that Theresa told me when I asked her how she could leave so many orphans behind when she could adopt only two.

I drove six hours across the Tennessee and North Carolina mountains to meet Theresa's orphans. I was never prepared for what I saw in who they were and what they are becoming. My life changed as their life does every day. Alan, pronounced A-LAN, is two, and Elena is thirteen. They were unrelated and from two different regions in Russia. Now, they are brother and sister. Theresa, my very good friend, is their mother and Keith their father. I am of Russian heritage; the orphans are Russian. Hence, our common background created a bond when we first met.

Theresa has soft green eyes and short blond hair. She is small and as sweet as the smell of honeysuckle. She found her children on the Internet. I don't know all of the details, but I do know that she prevailed through the mountain of paperwork, made a trip to Russia alone without speaking the language, stayed for twenty days within some of the most forbidding conditions, and came back with her two beautiful children. I watched her the week I was there and found her to be a most miraculous woman. Even though these children speak no English and she speaks no Russian, they talk and chatter all day with an understanding that convinces me that they have known each other for eons. Theresa found them again in this lifetime and has rescued them from the loveless street life of anonymity.

Theresa sets her alarm to get up at 1:00 AM, so she can awaken Elena to use the bathroom. Elena has a bed-wetting problem, and Theresa is going to break it in the gentlest way, the way of self-sacrifice. Elena had one pair of underwear in the orphanage. When she wet the bed, she would have to wash them in the morning and then put them back on for the day. They bathed once a week. She now bathes every morning before school. Elena is so happy when she does not wet the bed that it is a celebration. She wants very much to please her new mother. She wants to please.

Elena has deep blue eyes and pretty blond hair. Her smile is magical. It makes her eyes dance and sparkle. She throws her head back as her laughter comes from deep within. She and her sister went to a funeral with her mother when she was seven. Her mother left her children in the graveyard when the funeral was over and never came back for them. Elena went into the hospital for malnutrition and exposure. Her sister was separated from her and was adopted by a Russian couple. They never saw each other again. Elena moved from one orphanage to another as she grew into her thirteen years. I noticed that when Keith drives her to school, she sits in the back seat. He told me she won't sit in the front seat with him. He feels she is afraid of men. Theresa feels something happened to her in the orphanage that is inexplicable. It took a year before she sat in the front seat with Keith.

Her struggle for survival imbued her with the wisdom of an old woman. Behind her blue eyes, is the fear of having to move on again. She struggles every day to learn English, sit correctly, eat well, be helpful, and be pleasant. She shows only her best side and contains her emotion, which lies just beneath the surface of her lovely white skin, the cover for her soul.

One evening we were playing some CD's as Theresa was putting A LAN to bed. Elena began dancing. I have never seen such expression. She was fluid and graceful. Her eyes would close as the music surged through her. She lost herself for a moment within the passion of her people. When the music ended she looked shyly at me, not knowing if she had lost herself too much. When the next song began, I got up and danced. She saw my Russian passion, and then, she knew it was acceptable to express her emotion through music, the universal language. She began to dance again. She was angelic, as I imagine God's children are when we let them be.

A LAN was abandoned in the hospital after birth. He never knew a mother's touch. He went to an orphanage from the hospital. The back of his head is flat, caused by a vitamin D deficiency and where he lay in his bed without being touched or moved for long periods. He is so handsome, and his eyes so expressive. He is so alive and so active. He reaches for Theresa, and she picks him up in her arms, every time. He puts his arms around her neck and does not let go. He never lets her out of his sight. When she goes upstairs, he waits at the bottom for her with the most concerned look in his big brown eyes. I watched him and tears came to my eyes. I understood his fear and felt his nearly insatiable need for a loving touch, a hug and the reassurance that love gives. I assured him that she would be back, but he waited at the bottom, looking up and would not leave. He loves her and trusts her. When she gives him "time out" for misbehaving, he does not move from his seat. His eyes get very big, and he just waits quietly until his smile does her in. She is becoming immune to it in order to establish discipline in her household.

He learned how to smile in the orphanage, so he could survive the crush of all those around him. He has a beatific smile, and he uses it well. When he is scolded for a bad thing he has done or a good thing he has not done, he looks at Theresa and waits to calculate how serious he has to be. If he concludes that his deed is not a serious affront, he will smile. If the smile works, a small laughter grows into a big laughter as he moves into his seductive posture. He learned how to seduce the adults who had power over him. As an infant he could not walk; he could not talk, so he masterminded an offensive strategy to escape the harsh realities of being alone and defenseless. He had to be different, cute, playful, and alert. He learned his lessons well. He is all of those things and more.

When he first arrived in Theresa's household, he would make no noise. He ate voraciously, including the scraps that fell outside his plate. When food was removed from him, he screamed and cried. He did not talk much. He cautiously observed his new parents while evaluating his new position. I arrived one month later for my visit, and he chattered and shouted from the moment that he awoke until he went to nap at 12:00 pm and bed at 7:30 pm. Theresa's loving effect was opening him to the exploration of his self expression for the first time in his life.

One early morning, I found him in the kitchen sitting inside the open cabinet on the bottom shelf, with his feet on the floor as if it were his desk. He had Keith's cell phone and was talking to someone he imagined to be at the other end of the line. He shouted, then spoke quietly, then shouted again. On and on he went for at least thirty minutes. I watched and was amazed with his maturity and assumed authority. Theresa and I concluded that he was giving someone in his orphanage life a piece of his mind. When he finished, he was thoroughly satisfied, and we were amazed at his telephone skills.

He was acting out a scene he had seen many times in his young two years. How could he remember how to hold the phone, how to speak into it, and how to use his authoritative tone? What memory produced these skills? So many secrets, so many questions locked up within these two incredibly passionate Russian children. Where would one go to unlock the passageways into the complex maze of their early childhood experiences?

Theresa came to my guest room one evening to show me three pieces of clothing that her children were wearing when she received them. She asked the couriers if she could keep the clothes and was told to replace them with similar articles, as the orphanage could not afford to give them away. She gave the couriers some new clothing that she had brought with her for her new children. As she carefully unfolded the small, tattered, and shabby pieces, we wept. They had been worn until they had no color and no texture.

"Keep them as a remembrance of where they came from and where you are taking them", I said. "They will treasure these small things some day; it will be a link into their past. They must have a heritage; they must know where they came from. This will be their connection."

I thought of love. I watched the power of love in Theresa's household. I witnessed each day what love did to help these two children step quietly and slowly back into the innocence of childhood. I saw one foot fixed firmly into the present, not wanting

156

to let go of what they believed to be a final resting place for them. The other foot, which was planted in the past, was being loosened by the immeasurable capacity for love that Theresa and Keith displayed with their new children.

I thought of my own sons and how blessed they were. Their childhood always filled with love, physical attention, the concentration, and careful thought that went into developing their creative and intellectual capacities. I thought about the many times they reached to their father and me and how we reached back. I thought about our discipline and their tears. I thought about their eyes and how when they were young I saw the same looks of need and the looks of their small fears. I remembered their uncertainties and our reassurances. I thought of their clothes, their beds, and their toys. I saw the stuffed animals and smelled the clean sheets. I remembered the baths each night, the baby oil, the dinosaur pajamas. I thought of how important and significant they made my life and how much happiness they brought to their father's life. I thought of my own lost childhood and how I was able to recapture it with our sons. I thought of growing up and growing old with them and knew they would treasure us as we had treasured them. There is nothing in life more vital and fundamental than family. It is the source of who we are and what we value. It is what defines us.

As children reach for us, they reach into us. They stir our distant memories of a time when we reached towards love and reassurance. We all live forever with the memories of those who reached back, as they either stretched or diminished our capacity for love.

Love builds ladders that children quickly climb when they have lost time. Children are resilient, imaginative, and forgiving. They forget injustice in favor of growth. They have hope. They move on easily, but they do not forget their lessons. They carry their lessons throughout their lives. Some call these lessons "baggage". I call these lessons "life".

At the end of the day, we are all orphans. Those who brought us forth eventually depart, and when they leave us, we too are orphans. Most parents leave when we are adults, easing the passage for them to go. Some parents leave much earlier, and when they go, the innocence of their left behind children goes with them.

THE FAMILY

20. THE FAMILY

The center of the universe is filled with light. This light illuminates the darkest corners of space and time. It flows into all things that live. The assimilation of light brings forth life. All living things reach for light. No life exists without light.

The center of the universe is filled with love. It is there for all living things. This love waits for life to embrace it. Light gives us life, love nourishes it. No life is fulfilled without love.

We come from the light and are the family of man. The family is the center of each of our lives. We begin there, and we end there. It is our Family that picks us up for the first time, and it is our family that lays us down for the last time. This is where we grow, and this is where we are nourished. This is where we learn our lessons of light and love.

Life is filled with choices. These choices define our lives. Choices transport light or darkness. Our choices create a life of love or lovelessness. It is our parents who determine, by their action or inaction, the ability or inability for us to sustain light and love throughout our lives. They make our first choices when we are new, helpless, and seeking love. We trust them, and we believe them. They place our feet upon the path as we take our first steps. Their approval or disapproval establishes our values. We imitate them, because we want to be like them. They are our first heroes. They lead by example, and we follow. We rely upon their wisdom and life experiences to guide us. We look to our parents for vision. Their vision either limits or expands our lives. If they had parents without vision and they lacked the strength to climb up into the light; we will repeat what they know. It is the responsibility of each generation to improve the next. If this does not happen, then we remain as the generations who preceded us. Our parents determine whether we become beacons in the night or candles in the dark.

Parenting requires responsibility and sacrifice. We sacrifice our convenience, our time, and our material pleasures in our responsibility to cradle and nourish new life. Our children are innocent and pure when they arrive. They communicate with their cries of discomfort, hunger, and their need for big arms. They reach for us, and we reach back as family history repeats itself in this cycle of life. If no one reached for us when we reached for them, life's historical cycle may go unchanged instead of advancing. The children suffer as their potential is wasted in our inability to rise above our historical inadequacies and they become what they experience.

Children are dependent and filled with light. Every moment is new. Every object is wondrous. Every day is a first. They require time in their need for attention, reassurance, and direction. They are inquisitive and thirsty for answers. Our responses in their early childhood remain with them all of their lives as these responses fall upon open minds and open emotions. Parents till the garden and plant the seeds that grow to make our children the adults and the parents they become.

They crawl, then stand, then take their first steps, and then walk across a room. They cry, then scream, then speak their first word, and then say their first sentence. They hug our finger, then their bottle, then their teddy bear, and then they hug us. They look up at us one day and say, "love". I marvel at the complex tasks they learn in the first three short years they are alive. We do not master this much complexity for the rest of our adult lives. We build upon it. We become who reached back for us when we reached for them.

I did not want children. Now, I cannot live without them. They took me on the journey of a lifetime for a lifetime. They helped me to see myself. They taught me love and took me into the light when I was lost in the dark. They turned my candle into a beacon and allowed me to improve the next generation as my mother and father tried to improve theirs. We took this journey together, me with my vision and them with their trust.

I missed the Good Humor Man when my father became ill and ceased to be my father and I became his caretaker. We moved when I was a small child, and I often asked him in those days, "Daddy, whatever happened to the Good Humor Man?" He told me not to worry, that I would see him again someday. He was right I did find the Good Humor Men. They sold me dreamcicles and nourished every neglected corner of my life. They filled me.

We picked them up, and they will lay us down.

Children are for a lifetime.

IN CONCLUSION
AFTER THOUGHTS

I received much well-intended advice about how to raise our sons during my pregnancy and after they were born. I listened. I read books. I watched other parents. I tried to remember the best from my own childhood. I tried to imagine how a newborn baby experienced arriving out of the safe warm environment of the womb and into the life of new parents, in a strange place with strange noises. I wondered how they interpreted language and gestures and how difficult it had to be for them to communicate their needs in their complete dependency and helplessness. Their adjustments to climate, light, clothes, food, and the hundreds of foreign events each day seemed miraculous to me. They have no way of expressing their discomfort, confusion, or fear except through crying. Their joy is expressed in their contagious laughter, which fills us to the top and makes us laugh along with them. Their laughter is so pure that our laughter changes when we laugh with them. Listen.

Here is some of what I was told: get the name of a good babysitter; take a vacation with just you and your husband; put them in day care to have time for yourself and be sure to enroll them in preschool; don't pick them up every time they cry or they'll become spoiled; get them off the bottle as soon as possible so their teeth aren't ruined; potty train them or day care won't accept them; find a pediatrician in case they get sick; and use disposable diapers – not cloth diapers. These were a few of the litany of suggestions that became the struggle that conflicted with my intuition.

I tried to reconcile my common sense with the advice I received. When the time came to have our family, I could not ignore my instincts. We could not entrust our sons with those we did not know well so we had no babysitters. Our sons went with us when we took our vacations. It was easier than worrying about them. They did not attend day care where they would be influenced by the values of strangers. Instead, I invented my own preschool. Every time they cried, we picked them up. My mother used to say, "Babies cry when they are hungry, wet, or tired, and when they cry they want to be comforted". I know that when I cry I want to be comforted. It made sense to me.

They took a bottle until the day they threw it on the floor and said they did not want it anymore. They did not have cavities. I tried potty training Dmitri for about two days. It was so funny, and I laughed so hard trying to explain why he had to sit there that I gave up and figured that one day he would decide when he wanted real underpants. I was not about to force him to do something that I thought was a little ridiculous, and, because he did not go to day care, there was no pressing need to force this upon him until he was ready. One day he did ask me for underpants like 'dad wears' and that was that. His brother did the same.

We had a pediatrician for a while, and then, we did not have a pediatrician any more. They had their basic immunization shots, and when they got sick, which wasn't often, I doctored them with my grandmothers' and mothers' common sense, home remedies, and cures. I figured if it worked for me, it would work for them, and it did. We saved a lot of money, time, and the frustration of waiting to hear a doctor tell us what we already knew. I used diapers. I always liked the soft feel of cotton. I washed diapers every day but never had to deal with diaper rash or other problems that are associated with the convenience of synthetics. The power of love and commitment was demonstrated daily by decisions based upon common sense, intuition, and a strong desire to give the best we had to the most important decision we made, that of having children.

We wished for our sons to be successful in life and believed this would only be possible through their observing and experiencing actions of love. There is an old saying, "Believe what you see, not what you hear." It is what you see that makes the most vivid impressions in life. Words are worthless if they are not backed by action.

Success is not the accumulation of money, things, or titles. Success is defined by character. There is no way to fully assess the character of a child until they become adults. We plant seeds along the way of parenting and look for growth. We observe the results of their child rearing experiences as they grow toward adulthood. The evidence of these experiences is witnessed in their depth of compassion, intuition, understanding, tolerance, sacrifice, love, respect, loyalty, empathy, and commitment. Those who have these and other innumerable qualities, too subtle to list here, make us feel good when we are in their presence. They are unique adults and we treasure having known them.

We are only as deep and reflective as those who raised us. We love to the depth we were loved. The depth of our ability to love is the measure of our success, and this depth is what merits love from others. Character and its intricate integration and assimilation of these invaluable human qualities conquer adversity, and we flourish. Without character our light is as dim as a flickering candle, which from time to time blows out, requiring relighting in order to begin again. Authentic character, which has nothing to do with money or social status, is a beacon, not a candle. It is built upon the heroic blocks of conscientious, committed parenting.

ON EDUCATION, SOCIALIZATION, AND HOME SCHOOLING:

*"Children enter school as question marks
and leave as periods."*
Neil Postman, Educator

Public education does not teach creativity. Its focus is on the "right" answer. It teaches to the test. Children come up through a system where errors are to be avoided. Children are taught that right answers are rewarded and wrong answers have consequences. This philosophy of right and wrong is deeply rooted in the grading system. Children learn not to take risks for fear of failure. These inbred behavioral patterns lead to a life of accepting the one "right" answer. Our children lose the ability to search for more than one answer to a problem. We live in a highly competitive world and accepting only one answer sacrifices imagination and creativity, but worse, children lose their flexibility, which is a requirement for survival. "Nothing is more dangerous than an idea when it is the only one you have."

Children retain what is relevant to their lives. Adults do the same. It is imperative to emphasize creativity, flexibility, and imagination in the education of our children. Our schools teach children that the great ideas are the ideas that someone else has. When they learn this year after year they no longer believe they have the potential of having great ideas. These beliefs become their prisons where there are few jail breaks. Success and failure are believed to be opposites when, in fact, they are part of the same intellectual process of problem solving. In my own life failures served a useful purpose. They forced me to find new roads to travel where success was usually patiently waiting to be discovered.

It is imperative that children are released from this arcane method of education. Children meet your expectations, they don't know any better. They want to succeed. I taught a class once whose students were ranked as multilevel academic achievers. I prepared and taught as if they were all gifted students even though I knew many were not. Because I treated them as gifted, they responded as gifted. Many met the challenge and were proud of their achievements. This had a lasting effect upon them that year. They shifted their perspectives of who they were and what was possible for them to become.

Our home school emphasized a curriculum based upon the concept that every child is an artist who has a need to express himself; that each question may have more than one answer; that success and failure are part of the same process; that mistakes are positive because they encourage us to change direction; and, that work and play are the same.

We emphasized visual learning, learning through experience, and focusing on the positive aspects of new ideas for their interesting and useful applications. The school encouraged the creative experience in all subjects by having the children participate in the development of their learning. For example, math became a subject of relevance when they designed, specified, and constructed their tree house. Children learn and retain what has relevant purpose in their lives.

When we began the Children's School, we were told that our children would not be properly socialized. That was a ridiculous notion to me, as I knew that babies, toddlers, and young children

168

want their moms and dads to be surrounding them, not strangers who have no vested emotional interest in them. Imagine day care at birth or as toddlers. At this point in a child's life, their minds are like sponges as they soak in everything around them. Better to soak in the love and devotion of parents rather than experience the emotional neglect of strangers. Imagine having to compete as a toddler with children who are older. Imagine crying for hours as a baby and no one picking you up, because there are many other distractions in need of attention.

Our sons did not get socialized in those ways. They did have great conversations with us, their parents, with family friends, with our business associates. They were entertained and were very entertaining in all the places they traveled on our wonderful family holidays. They mingled mostly with adults many of whom loved children. Hence, they experienced happy acceptance and genuine affection during their early years of 'socialization'. Speaking to them today, one would never know they were deprived the socialization of their peers at the ages of infant, toddler, and small child.

In an uncertain world, children are anchored and comforted by tradition and activities. Parents are their first and best teachers. They are their social experience in their young, innocent lives.

Because we lived in the mountains, we had few close neighbors. Our community was spread over long distances. We had no neighborhood. Mountain fun and education into life comes mostly from nature, animals, and common sense. There are few external distractions as many children have in small communities and cities. We made our own distractions, which were centered on family events and the length of the day. Spring and summer were outside activities, fall and winter, with its short days, were inside activities. We had to be creative to keep their young minds moving forward.

If we had a neighborhood, as exists in many small towns and cities throughout this great country, I might have banded together with my neighbors who had small children. I might have organized my neighborhood into a community of educators, all of us teaching from our various levels of expertise. I might have helped to create home schooling activities in our garages and homes that educated and inspired the creativity of each child. All of us might have participated and shared in the experience of teaching and stimulating the creative expression of our neighborhood children. Our "family" might have been large and diverse. We all could have schooled our neighborhood children. The possibilities could have been endless, had I lived in a neighborhood community. All things are possible with imagination. Anyone could do this and maybe we should all try.

ON FAMILY:

I think that raising children depends on common sense and a strong desire to succeed in the most important event in a marriage, childbirth. We have a way of casually justifying the neglect we impose upon the innocent. We give birth, and then we go away from nourishing the brain development of our most precious creations. Our busy lives convince us they don't need us, so we farm them out to strangers to raise in the day time hours. We try and fit our children into the leftover spaces of our lives in the after hours, and they grow up unable to define their value.

It does not take much investigation to see the failure of the American family and the neglect of their children. Just go to any mall in America on any day after school, and you will see all of the dislocated children wandering around looking for purpose and meaning. You cannot miss seeing them, because they all look alike, embracing sameness and terrified of being different. They are afraid of defining themselves, and this may be because they were never provided the tools with which to do this. They come from places where they are forced to conform in order to fit. Individualism is not celebrated. Intelligence is not praised. Talent is not admired.

How have we come to this when we came from a generation that raised us in strong family units where we were cuddled at birth, hugged, kissed, spanked, applauded, and where our individuality was encouraged, or at the least tolerated? Family took care of all of us from the corner grocer to the favorite aunt. Many eyes were always on us.

The evening meal was the time when families came together to share their day, to express their problems, to define solutions and to bond in love. Family love reinforced our individual worth. To be sure, we all had our insecurities but those did not out run our boundaries. We knew we would be rescued if we fell into trouble, but it had better not be 'Bad Trouble'. We always knew we had a destiny, and that defined destiny was to be greater than our parents. The goal was higher education and there could be no excuses because our parents sacrificed daily so we could meet that goal. We saw it and we did all we could to deliver.

Sadly, these extended families, that used to live in the same or surrounding neighborhoods dispersed. Even though we have broken up and separated, there are ways to create families out of neighborhoods of diversity. It takes character, creativity, and spontaneity. It is worth the journey, but it means leaving preconceived notions behind and opening frontiers in our thinking. Americans love frontiers and covered wagons. They love cowboys and the Wild West. They thirst for adventure and the unknown as the monotony of their repetitive existence dulls their edge. They live vicariously in front of their TV's as they sit in their living rooms thinking they have no way to get there from here. They become the examples for their children.

We can do this. We can educate and stimulate the creative spirit in our children. We can encourage their individuality and uniqueness. It involves sacrifice and selflessness, but the rewards are immeasurable and priceless when our sons and daughters become more than we are. They become our legacy.

ON FINISHING:

If we thought it to start it, we finished it. No project, no idea, no commitment went incomplete. We saw it through to the end even when we lost interest, were tired, distracted, discouraged, or just didn't want to do it anymore. We finished when obstacles were overwhelming and when others turned back. We finished when we were told we couldn't, especially when we were told we couldn't. Never lie down, always get up. Fall but don't falter. Stay focused when life blurs.

Finishing requires determination, and determination requires commitment. If it gets too tough, too hot, too controversial, too expensive, too long, too arduous, too risky, too uncomfortable, many quit. They never know what the end looked like, or if they could have finished. They never know their limitations or their levels of endurance. They live a life of ambiguity never understanding where they could have gone. They settle for mediocrity with excuses.

We four walked in the rain, so we could see the sun come out. We climbed the mountain, so we could see the valley. We were cold, so we could feel the heat of the fire. We worked until covered in sweat, so we could taste a fresh shower. We witnessed birth and knew death. We experienced bigotry, so we could understand tolerance. We learned how to finish by appreciating human diversity and the power of nature.

Each finish has its rewards and losses. It is worth the journey in knowing who we are and how we've changed when we finish. Many begin and end early without knowing where they could have been. Our children should know where they are and how they got there. They learn this by finishing everything they begin no matter the course or the obstacles. They should all cross the finish line for the exhilaration of having done the impossible. Finishing changes a child for life.

ON ART AND MUSIC:

What humanizes us? What helps us understand our personal dimensions? What liberates our energy and vitality? What stirs our profound insights into passion and imagination? Why have our children in this culture disappeared? Where have they gone and why did they leave?

I do not have the answers to these questions, only my suspicions. I suspect they left when the music stopped playing.

They are the first ones we sacrifice when times get tough. Walk through our schools. Gather up some friends and walk through your schools. Look at the rooms, the paint, the desks, the instructors, the food, the playground, the curriculum, the instructional materials and aids, and the faces in the halls as they walk past your group. Then ask yourself, would I want to spend eight hours here in this place, five days a week?

What do we expect these children to become in these sub standard facilities that require everyone to become standard? How do we expect our children to thrive and flourish in a place that, by its falling apart, communicates to them they are worthless? They know they are the last priority on the list.

We cut budgets to keep schools functioning, if that is what we call it. Our teachers' salaries are equal to our respect for them. These silent attitudes are communicated to our children. Their disrespect for these professional warriors creates an atmosphere of havoc in classrooms where order should prevail. We are all punished.

The first curriculum cuts come in music and art, which are the subjects that stir the chords of a child's creativity. The last cuts are athletics, where the few participate for the glory of admiring fans and the promise of athletic scholarships.

English is a required course for all three years of high school, at least when I looked the last time, and many students are unable to express themselves articulately in the English language. They pride themselves on their accomplished level of slang language, without realizing how this marks them for life in a world that is only growing more competitive. Many are unable to write a coherent paragraph. Composition and fluent self expression are not considered required accomplishments for the masses we process through our public educational system.

Art and Music are electives or extracurricular activities, if they exist in the school. They are not required. Art liberates the soul of self expression. It ignites creativity. I have seen children filled with pride when their first painting resembles something they recognize and recreated from their imagination. They want to gift it to their parents to hang on the wall. We deny every child this experience of pride and self acknowledgement when we take art from them. We deny them recognition and a peek into their soul. We make their light dimmer and they lose their way into who they are. Creativity and self expression are irreplaceable losses for a child. Why do we take this from them?

Music is rhythm and math. When a child learns music he is building a base for math. Half notes, quarter notes, sixteenth, thirty seconds, measures, counting, adding, hesitation, length of a chord, and on and on. When a child learns music he is learning a universal language that is understood by everyone in the world. He can lay his violin case in the street and play for money, all will understand from Budapest to Beijing. He will never starve because everyone loves music. Children in music classes become excited and joyful when they play an instrument that resonates and harmonizes with everyone around them. They are accomplished.

It stirs something deep inside that is difficult to define. I call it passion. Who can sit at a concert and feel nothing? Who can listen to a CD and feel nothing? Music sustains passion in a child, and this is what we cut from our curriculum?

I don't get it. What happened to common sense and sensitivity? How can we proclaim to care so much for our children and our schools, and do so little? They get it. They know. They do not listen to what we say; they watch what we do.

Because we do not revere education in this country, our children will become the worker bees for those who are educated in countries where education is valued and accomplishment is esteemed. We have dumbed down our children, their standards, and in the end, the quality of their lives. All this for budget cuts, money; all for paper. It can be torn into pieces. It burns.

ON FAMILY VALUE COMPATIBILITY:

Recently I received an email from a friend. It was lengthy, however, one section of this thought provoking email caught my attention:

*"We ate cupcakes, white bread and real butter and drank Kool-aid made with sugar, but we weren't overweight because, **WE WERE ALWAYS OUTSIDE PLAYING!***

We would leave home in the morning and play all day, as long as we were back when the streetlights came on.

No one was able to reach us all day... And we were OK.

We would spend hours building our go-carts out of scraps and then ride down the hill, only to find out we forgot the brakes. After running into the bushes a few times, we learned to solve the problem.

174

We did not have Playstations, Nintendo's, X-boxes, no video games at all, no 150 channels on cable, no video movies or DVD 's, no surround-sound or CD's, no cell phones, no personal computers, no Internet or chatrooms! **WE HAD FRIENDS because we went outside and found them!**

We fell out of trees, got cut, broke bones and teeth and there were no lawsuits from these accidents. We ate worms and mud pies made from dirt, and the worms did not live in us forever.

We were given BB guns for our 10th birthdays, made up games with sticks and tennis balls and although we were told it would happen, we did not poke out very many eyes. We rode bikes or walked to a friend's house and knocked on the door or rang the bell, or just walked in and talked to them!

Little League had tryouts and not everyone made the team. Those who didn't had to learn to deal with disappointment. Imagine that!!

The idea of a parent bailing us out if we broke the law was unheard of. They actually sided with the law!

These generations have produced some of the best risk-takers, problem solvers and inventors ever! The past 50 years have been an explosion of innovation and new ideas.

We had Freedom, Failure, Success and Responsibility, and we learned HOW TO DEAL WITH IT ALL!"

Anonymous

We were outside playing because our parents did not spend money on distractions for us. They worked hard, came home tired and expected us to create our own amusements. We ate everything we could get our hands on and did not get fat. The word obese was unknown. Our mothers cooked 3 meals a day; breakfast before school, packed a school lunch with a sandwich, fruit and a bag of chopped raw vegetables, and we all sat down together for the evening meal, no excuses. We all had vegetable gardens even though we lived in a city and going to a restaurant was only for a special occasion. We thought fast food was a meal our mothers cooked fast.

We were taught respect for our elders and when given a curfew, we showed up. We respected money and the importance it had on our family survival and comfort. We invented our games from scraps and our imaginations, and they cost nothing. They gave us great joy, pride of ownership, lots of exercise, and when we went to bed we were totally tired.

We did fall out of trees, get cut and skinned our knees. The band aid and iodine were our home remedies and could be found in the bathroom medicine cabinet above the sink. When we went there to help 'doctor' ourselves there were no prescription drugs, just a bottle of aspirin.

Our bicycles were the most important gift we could receive. It was freedom! We rode everywhere. We did deal with our disappointments and rejections and this made us stronger and more determined to succeed. Our parents did believe the teachers when they sent home a note with us. Discipline was swift and final. Teachers did not have to send home a second note.

I realize that times have changed. The digital age has brought wonderful and exhilarating devices that make all of our lives personally and professionally interesting and efficient. However, there is no need to sacrifice discipline, respect, commitment, integrity and family values for progress. They are compatible. THEY ARE COMPATIBLE!

These values are more important now than ever before. As the world grows more competitive and as populations explode, these family values will be what keep us civilized and humane. We are only able to treat others to the level we were treated and to the level of how we value ourselves. Values are instilled in early childhood and practiced throughout our growing up and into our adult life. We must treasure them. They are what will save us from ourselves.

ON DISCIPLINE, AKA LOVE:

Children want to be loved. They want to be accepted. They are small and innocent with no life experiences when they come to us. They define love and acceptance by the amount of attention we pay to them. When they stray, we discipline them and return them to the path. Children connect discipline to love. Discipline requires parental observation and involvement. It requires time. Children love attention, and our time, and they do the damndest things to get it, repeatedly.

When we reach down and lift them up, they know we care. Discipline is security, and it teaches boundaries. All children need boundaries. I remember a trip to Eastern Europe where my friend took along her small child, maybe two years old. The child ran the mother's life during the trip. She was unruly, selfish, undisciplined, disruptive, and unwelcome in many places. I looked at the child and the mother one night after the child threw a tantrum that disrupted the conversation of our hosts and said quietly and firmly, "We ran the children in our household, they did not run us." I made my point, and I lost a friend.

Why do parents fear their children? Do they think their disruptive children are acceptable? Rude, undisciplined children are rejected and in some instances merely tolerated until they go away. They are not invited back. Parents who neglect their responsibilities in establishing values and boundaries set their children up for rejection and ridicule. They clear their path for failure.

Children know when they are not loved. Love is the most important thing to them, and their whole focus is upon achieving it from their parents. Unloved children are easy to spot as adults. They are the ones we avoid, the ones we leave out, the ones we reject. They struggle to achieve love in the ways demonstrated to them by their parents. When it becomes illusive, they become disruptive adults, just as they were as children. They humiliate themselves in their search for love. Under their façade at the end of the day, their dim light burns out, and they are alone, outside where their parents left them years ago.

Parenting is a full-time job.

"There are no short cuts to any place worth going."

ACKNOWLEDGEMENTS

I would like to thank every individual who spent time with me in my life. Their collective energy, whether it was positive or negative, provided the steps to the ladder upon which I climbed. I learned a life lesson from each person and those lessons combined to make me the woman I am today. I could not have done it without them.

Thank you GunnMen for your faith, laughter, humor, tears, compassion, intensity, love, intellect, and creativity. Thank you for the many challenges you tossed in my direction. Some were profound, some painful, some joyful, most loving – all were worth the journey.

The Children's School thanks its teacher, Nancy York, whose commitment and energy laid the foundation for the intellectual discipline and success of our sons. The School thanks our karate instructor, Phil Little; a 10th degree black belt and International Grandmaster, whose intensity and devotion to Isshinryu gave our sons the balance they would call upon many times in their lives. We thank Victoria Boone, Sandy Blaine and the many participating artists, too numerous to name here, for their huge creative spirit and love of children. They taught oil and acrylic painting, clay, pottery, silk screen printing, photography, line drawing, sculpture, weaving, macramé, paper making, water colors, charcoal, and many other art skills. They gave our sons perception, depth, and color. Because of these amazing artists our sons' lives will never be gray. We posthumously thank Lev and Galina Belenky for their extraordinary musical talents, character, and ability to create superior musicians of all their students. Many went on to win serious music competitions to the honor of their teachers.

Thank you Lillian Rogosdik for answering my ad in the New York Times. You pushed two small boys to finishing every art project they began. Your wonderful French accent, fresh garden cooking, and unconditional love for our sons instilled in them an amazing depth of confidence and acceptance. We miss you to this day.

Thank you Debra Gaynor and Rita Pistorio for your indomitable spirit and belief in this book, for your editorial comments that improved its content, and for never giving up on this project. Thank you James Ventrillo for your guidance through the publication process and for sharing your experience and knowledge. Thank you Pam Winterbottom for your extraordinary illustrations and book cover. Your understanding of the childlike mind brought my book to life and gave it color. A special thanks to Dick Davis, PhD, for approval to use his translated version of the quote from "The Little Virtues" by Natalia Ginsburg.

Many thanks to those who took the time to read the drafts and make your valuable comments; Ani Chang, Sherry Bellamy, Patricia Acton, Kate Gardner, Joan Swenson, Betsy Lewis, and Stephen Gunn.

Thank you Dmitri Gunn for always being there throughout this long process and for understanding what this meant to me on a profound spiritual level. When I would begin to lose heart you would remind me, "Remember what the Japanese did after World War II? They picked themselves up, dusted themselves off and sold us Sony, Mitsubishi, Honda, Hitachi, Nikon, Yamaha, and Panasonic."

*"Those who say it can't be done
should get out of the way of those who are doing it."*

I hope you have enjoyed this book. It took a lifetime to write.
I had to grow up before I could begin.

Please visit the following website to learn more about creative
parenting and to interact with the author who is available for
seminars and speaking engagements:

www.peekabooparenting.com

The 20 illustrations in this book are available as color prints*, which
are suitable for framing. They showcase the creativity of children's
imaginations. Please visit the website to view the illustrations in
color along with pricing and shipping information.

* In order for this book to be affordable, we made the difficult
artistic decision to print the illustrations in black and white.

www.ingramcontent.com/pod-product-compliance
Lightning Source LLC
Chambersburg PA
CBHW070958040426
42443CB00007B/564